MANDELA

MANDELA

Charlene Smith

Foreword by Archbishop Desmond Tutu

JOHNNIC

First published in 1999 by Struik Publishers (Pty) Ltd
(a member of Struik New Holland Publishing (Pty) Ltd)
Registration number 54/00965/07

London • Cape Town • Sydney • Auckland

24 Nutford Place
London W1H 6DQ
United Kingdom

80 McKenzie Street
Cape Town 8001
South Africa

14 Aquatic Drive
Frenchs Forest
NSW 2086, Australia

218 Lake Road
Northcote, Auckland
New Zealand

2 4 6 8 10 9 7 5 3 1

Managing editor: Annlerie van Rooyen
Designer: Janice Evans
Editor: Lesley Hay-Whitton
Picture researcher: Carmen Watts
Proofreader: Annelene van der Merwe
Indexer: Gill Gordon

ISBN 1 86872 206 6

Reproduction by Hirt & Carter Cape (Pty) Ltd
Printed and bound by Tien Wah Press (Pte.) Ltd, Singapore

PUBLISHERS' NOTES

• All efforts have been made to ascertain people's names.
These have been omitted where no reliable sources could be found.
• The opinions expressed in this book are those of the author and do
not necessarily reflect the opinions of the publisher.
• The terms 'black' and 'African' refer to all people that were not
born with white skins. However, in this book, to explain certain
peculiarities of laws or events, or in quoting sources directly, the
terms 'coloured' or 'Indian' are on occasion used.

PAGE 1: The 'Madiba jive'.
· PAGES 2 AND 3: Nelson Mandela in the Franschhoek Valley.
*THIS PAGE: Nelson Mandela and Walter Sisulu while imprisoned on
Robben Island (top); Nelson Mandela and Graça Machel at a 'Culture
of Learning' campaign function in Soweto (bottom).*

Contents

JOHNNIC

President Nelson Mandela told the Joint Houses of the Congress of the United States of America on 6 October 1994: 'At the end the overwhelming majority, both black and white, decided to invest in peace.' An investment in peace and national reconciliation led by President Nelson Rolihlahla Mandela at his inauguration in May 1994 as South Africa's first democratic president provided a unique testimony to the world that swords were indeed of greater use as ploughshares, that negotiation was a greater and more effective triumph than war. The South African economy rewarded this approach with a sustained climb and greater stability under Mandela's time in office, despite stormy global markets.

Nelson Mandela led by example. It was his profound belief that political liberation was empty without economic liberation. With these tenets in mind Johannesburg Consolidated Investment Company Limited, a leading South African conglomerate, was at the instance of its major shareholder, Anglo American Corporation Limited, unbundled in 1995. As a result, Johnnies Industrial Corporation Limited (Johnnic) and JCI Limited (JCI) came into being, and the controlling stakes therein were made available to black investors.

The vision that led to the unbundling was spurred by Mandela's call for economic liberation through the creation of black economic empowerment groups. The National Empowerment Consortium (NEC), a partnership between trade unions, investment companies and black business groups acquired a 35% stake in Johnnic, benefiting three million new investors who took control of the R10 billion conglomerate.

When he spoke to the US Congress in 1994, Mandela noted: 'As the images of life lived anywhere on the globe become available to all, so will the contrast between rich and the poor within and across frontiers, and within and across continents, become a motivating force impelling the deprived to demand a better life. As the possibility of nations to become islands, sufficient unto themselves, diminishes and vanishes forever, so will it be that the suffering of the one shall, at the same time, inflict pain upon the other.' He said that this may mean that technology will do what all the great thinkers failed to do – prove that 'we are all part of one, indivisible and common humanity'.

Johnnic as a leader in telecommunications, media and entertainments recognises these challenges. It has a vision of leading the African renaissance in media and communications, taking with it the diversified talent, skills and cultures of a remarkable continent.

Johnnic joins all South Africans in wishing the greatest figure of the twentieth century, and the greatest African of the millennium, *Hambakahle*. It has been an honour to be led by a figure who embodies the triumph of the human spirit, a liberator for all humankind.

Acknowledgements

This book is in many ways drawn from my experiences over two decades of political journalism in South Africa, of many inspiring people and important events I have been privileged to report on or be a part of. Over time I became convinced of the value of listening to the wisdom of ordinary people, and of trying to write in ways that would have meaning to their lives, while recognising the imperatives of history and democracy. The liberation struggle did not end with the first democratic elections in 1994, it continues as the struggle for economic justice, without which democracy cannot survive.

Many folk contributed valuable time to help me, and I thank them. I salute the custodians and workers at two national treasures, both endangered because of financing cuts: the invaluable Mayibuye Centre at the University of the Western Cape and the South African National Library in Cape Town. My children Leila and Matthew remain my inspiration, as does my extended family, Franklin Sekonya, Abie Makhura, Dale, Myles and Kate Harris, Morné Davids, Bethuel, Gloria and Nhlanhla Nkosi. Their sensitivity to making South Africa a great society, free of racial prejudice and class consciousness, fills me with respect.

My publishers Struik are dream publishers. They put up with my foibles and show caring in aspects of my private life where they need not. Without the nurturing of this anxious writer by Annlerie van Rooyen, no books could emerge. I have a great debt of gratitude to her. Janice Evans astounds me with her brilliant book designs. My editor Lesley Hay-Whitton had a fine sense for detail that, despite my griping, I appreciate. Lois O'Brien and Alasdair Verschoyle showed encouragement in every way imaginable. Viva Struik.

This book is critical of Mandela in some respects, but it was important to tell young people of this land that he is not a saint: they can all aspire to greatness if they have commitment. It is a mark of the man that he said, 'Judge me not by my success, but on how many times I have fallen and risen'. Nothing is impossible if you are determined. A dream has to be born.

My first meeting with Mandela was on the third day of his release when I interviewed him for *Business Day* at his home in Orlando West. Then, and later, I was struck by his extraordinary warmth and careful consideration of every question. Mandela, more than any other leader I have met, has the air of a person who knows he was born to greatness. He has a regal air combined with a sensitivity that is overwhelming. In societies where class makes some people (security guards, cleaners, waiters) 'invisible', and where most fail to acknowledge their presence, Mandela will clasp them by the hand and stop to ask about their lives. Every ordinary person who has met Mandela has been made to feel special by him.

What of our fears about 'after Mandela goes'? I wonder if Mandela will ever leave us. He showed great wisdom in handing over most of the reins of government to Thabo Mbeki during his last years in office, allowing Mbeki to make mistakes – the Mandela icon could shield South Africa from many small errors. Mbeki is a man too with a dream. He is determined to be one of Africa's great leaders and to make South Africa one of the world's great nations.

I believe we will look back at this time and say Mandela brought the start of South Africa's golden age, but it will not end with him – that is his great gift, and our remarkable fortune.

CHARLENE SMITH

I come from a culture where traditionally, children are seen as both our present and our future, so I have always believed it is our responsibility as adults to give children futures worth having.

GRAÇA MACHEL
REPORT ON THE IMPACT
OF ARMED CONFLICT ON CHILDREN,
UNITED NATIONS, 1996

OPPOSITE PAGE, FROM LEFT: Nelson Mandela and Graça Machel, widow of the Mozambican president Samora Machel; Nelson and Graça were married on his eightieth birthday on 18 July 1998. Nelson Mandela casts his vote during South Africa's first democratic elections in 1994. The President always took time to make everyone feel special.

Foreword

In July 1988, two years before Nelson Mandela walked a free man from Victor Verster prison, Archbishop Trevor Huddleston suggested, in his role as the President of the Anti-Apartheid Movement, that the world should celebrate Mandela's 70th birthday in prison. Many thousands of young people especially, although not exclusively, responded enthusiastically to his call to make this the mother of all birthday celebrations. People of all ages went on pilgrimage from all the corners of the United Kingdom and then they gathered at Hyde Park Corner in London, an enormous sea of faces. They congregated there, 250,000 of them, and the vast majority were young people.

What struck me forcibly, as I gazed over them, was that most of them had not even been born when Madiba was sentenced to life imprisonment in 1963, and they had not seen him since; they had not heard from him, but they had certainly heard about him from others. The point is that they had no direct knowledge of him and, since pictures of prisoners were not permitted, they did not know what he really even looked like now. And yet here they were paying tribute to a prisoner, yes a prisoner, of conscience whom the British Minister Margaret Thatcher of the time had disdainfully dismissed as a terrorist.

What an extraordinary phenomenon that he was able to move people so deeply without saying anything, without doing anything. Some of us worried that they might be in for an enormous disillusionment, that they would discover that their idol had feet of clay. Perhaps it would be better that he should remain incarcerated, out of sight, because distance did indeed lend enchantment to the view. In prison he was serving a splendid purpose because he was giving focus to the struggle, personalizing it in that way so essential for causes if they were to galvanize the kind of popular support that the largely indifferent Reagan White House and Thatcher 10 Downing Street would find difficult to ignore. Outside prison he would be found to be less effective because he would be so human, so vulnerable, so disappointing to those who had placed him on a pedestal of near sainthood and infallibility.

Yes, we were all in the seventh heaven of delight on 11 February 1990, when he walked out of Victor Verster prison side by side with Winnie. It was an unforgettable day, but there were butterflies in the pit of the stomach – would he measure up to all that people believed and hoped about him? Would we not all come crashing to the ground after all the euphoria? The world joined us in welcoming the world's most famous prisoner, but for how long would they pay attention when they are so notoriously fickle? Was he but a few days' wonder and would they flit off to the next attraction to land in their spotlight?

The man is a phenomenon, in a class by himself, for the frenzy of media attention has not abated. If anything, it has increased. Far from being a huge disillusionment, he has not ceased to amaze everyone. A deeply divided land, alienated by long years of repression and injustice, and at variance on most subjects, is unanimous about one thing: that this former terrorist, so frequently vilified and hated, is today our greatest asset.

He is loved by virtually all South Africans, even the most virulent critics of his ANC-led government. He is the most popular political leader in the land, almost beyond criticism. Who will easily forget the scenes at Ellis Park when he walked onto the turf wearing François Pienaar's No. 6 on his Springbok jersey on the day of the final for the Rugby World Cup in 1995, when an overwhelmingly white crowd, mostly Afrikaners, broke out in reverberating chants: 'Nelson, Nelson, Nelson'. He has the knack of doing the right thing, which with some political leaders would be contrived or gauche. With him it turns out to be exactly what touches responsive chords in the people. He has bowled South Africans and indeed the world over with his extraordinary magnanimity, his readiness and eagerness to forgive. He invited the widows of former South African political leaders of all persuasions and races to a tea party at the Presidency and charmed them off their feet. He stole the hearts of many Afrikaners, whom he had already attracted by supporting the Springbok emblem for rugby, by going to visit the widow of Dr Verwoerd in her Afrikaner exclusivist stronghold – Orania. Here he was having tea, at some inconvenience to himself, with the widow of the architect and high priest of apartheid. Unbelievable! He later had a meal with Dr Percy Yutar, the man who had prosecuted in the Rivonia Trial and who many believed had gone well beyond the accepted conventions in passionately demanding the death sentence for the accused. His magnanimity knows no bounds. He was ready to have accompanied Mr PW Botha to appear before the TRC as subpoenaed, if it would help Mr Botha not feel humiliated.

An interesting mix of genuine humility and a regal sense of his position, he is at pains to say he is no saint and just an ordinary member of the ANC, a consensus man. And he can appear in court because he has a high sense of the law and stood for two days to demonstrate that respect. But he can be short with those who are presumptuous with regard to his office, not his person. He undoubtedly is our greatest gift and asset. God blessed us wonderfully in giving him to us at this period in our history – he has helped to hold together a fractious lot. God's sense of humour is huge. Here is the terrorist par excellence whom some of the high and mighty in former days spurned. Now everyone rushes to South Africa on state or other visits, just to have a photo opportunity with the world's most admired statesman. Some people might want the earth to open up so that their leaders might disappear out of sight – we stand tall because we have a transparently good man as our President.

A European Prime Minister urged me to try to get Mandela to visit his country to say farewell. I know many other countries would consider it a great honour if he came before his retirement. No-one else that I know as head of state has been asked to so many regional summits to take leave of his fellow heads of state in Europe, Africa, Latin America and Asia.

He has left us a wonderful legacy – to strive to become increasingly one people with diverse cultures, languages, beliefs of different races and so on – the rainbow people of South Africa – and we owe him an enormous debt of gratitude. He has laid a good and firm foundation. It is up to all of us to make sure we build a structure that will stand the buffetings of fate. That would be the only fitting monument to him.

ARCHBISHOP DESMOND TUTU, 1998

Archbishop Desmond Tutu and the newly elected President, Nelson Mandela, in 1994: comrades in truth.

Mandela's life

1918
JULY 18: A son, Nelson Rolihlahla, is born to Chief Gadla Henry Mphakan-yiswa and his third wife, Nosekeni Fanny, at the village of Mvezo in Transkei (Eastern Cape).

1927
Chief Gadla dies and Nelson is taken into the care of his uncle Chief Jon-gintaba Dalindyebo, acting regent of the Thembu. Jongintaba has a profound effect on Mandela's life, sending him to good missionary schools and giving him a thorough grounding in Xhosa culture, history and the duties implicit in governing.

1930s
Mandela begins his university education at Fort Hare.

1940s
Mandela, fleeing a planned marriage in Transkei, goes to Johannesburg. He becomes articled as a legal clerk and continues his studies at the University of the Witwatersrand. He qualifies and marries Evelyn Ntoko Mase. They have four children – two sons, Thembi and Makgatho, and Maki (their first daughter, also called Maki, died in infancy).

1952
Mandela and Oliver Tambo set up Johannesburg's first black law firm. JUNE 26: Campaign for the Defiance of Unjust Laws is launched by the African National Congress (ANC) and the SA Indian Congress, with Mandela as volunteer in chief. Volunteers imprisoned for defying apartheid legislation.

1953
Mandela and Walter Sisulu begin discussing the feasibility of armed action. Mandela and Evelyn separate.

1955
Mandela meets a young social worker, Winnie Nomzamo Madikizela. JUNE 26: Freedom Charter adopted.

1956
Mandela and 155 others are arrested. During the four-year Treason Trial the State fails to prove the Freedom Charter is a communist document.

1958
Mandela and Evelyn are divorced. JUNE 14: He and Winnie marry.

1959
FEBRUARY 5: A daughter, Zenani, is born to Nelson and Winnie.

1960
The ANC is banned. DECEMBER 23: A second daughter, Zindzi Mandela, is born.

1961–63
DECEMBER 16 1961: Launch of Umkhonto we Sizwe (MK), the ANC's armed wing. Mandela goes underground in 1961, travels abroad in 1962 and receives military training in Algeria and in Ethiopia. On his return to South Africa in 1962, he is convicted of leaving the country illegally and inciting workers to strike. He is serving this sentence when on 11 July 1963 police raid Lilliesleaf farm in Rivonia, Johannesburg. MK High Command is arrested. The Rivonia Trial sees Mandela and his comrades sentenced to life imprisonment for sabotage.

1964
Mandela is transferred with the other black Rivonia Trialists from Pretoria Local prison to Robben Island.

1968
Mandela's mother dies.

1969
Mandela's elder son, Thembi, dies in a car accident at the age of 25.

1982
APRIL: Mandela, Walter Sisulu, Ahmed Kathrada, Raymond Mhlaba and Andrew Mlangeni are moved from Robben Island to Pollsmoor prison in Cape Town.

1983
Minister of Prisons Louis le Grange visits Mandela and appoints prison chief Brigadier Aucamp as go-between between him and government.

1984
MAY: For the first time in 21 years Mandela is allowed to have a contact visit with Winnie.

NOVEMBER: Mandela is separated from other prisoners as tentative steps toward negotiations between Mandela and government begin.

1985
JANUARY 31: President PW Botha tells parliament he will release Mandela if he rejects violence. Mandela responds by saying government must reject violence first.

1986
Government hints that Mandela will be released in return for the release of jailed Soviet dissidents in Russia.

1988
DECEMBER: Mandela, after recovering from tuberculosis, is transferred to Victor Verster prison in Paarl, where private meetings with government representatives can be held.

1989
JULY 5: Outgoing President PW Botha meets Mandela at Tuynhuys, Cape Town.

1990
FEBRUARY 11: Mandela is released. He returns to Soweto two days later.

1991
JANUARY 29: Mandela and Buthelezi discuss ways to find peace in KwaZulu-Natal. APRIL 4: Mandela tells the ANC National Executive Committee meeting that he was wrong to call De Klerk a 'man of integrity'. APRIL 5: The ANC delivers an ultimatum to De Klerk to take steps to end violence or talks will cease. JUNE: Nelson Mandela is elected ANC president as an ailing Oliver Tambo steps down. DECEMBER 20–21: Convention for a Democratic SA (Codesa) begins. De Klerk delivers a broadside on the ANC and Mandela lashes back.

1992
APRIL 13: Mandela announces his separation from his wife Winnie. They are divorced four years later. SEPTEMBER 26: Mandela and De Klerk sign a Record of Understanding to get negotiations back on the table – and to curb violence.

1994
APRIL 26: Mandela leads his people in voting for the first time in their lives by casting his first vote at the age of 75. MAY 10: Nelson Mandela is inaugurated as South Africa's first black President with Thabo Mbeki and FW de Klerk as his deputy presidents.

1997
DECEMBER: Mandela steps down as ANC president. A year before he had begun relinquishing many duties to Thabo Mbeki to prepare him for running the ANC and South Africa.

1998
JULY 18: On his eightieth birthday Mandela marries Graça Machel, the widow of one of the ANC's closest allies, Mozambican President Samora Machel. When the couple tour the world bidding farewell to world leaders, Mandela is showered with the highest honours that most countries can award.

1999
FEBRUARY 5: President Mandela's final opening of parliament. MARCH 26: President Mandela formally hands over the reins to his successor, Thabo Mbeki.

OPPOSITE PAGE, CLOCKWISE FROM TOP LEFT: Mandela grew a beard during the period he spent underground (1961 to 1962) and was known as the 'Black Pimpernel'. Mandela greets people of the Mitchells Plain community near Cape Town. Wearing sunglasses to protect his eyes from the limestone that damaged them while he was incarcerated on Robben Island, Nelson Mandela chips at limestone for press photographers on a revisit in 1994. An exuberant Nelson and Winnie Mandela after their wedding in 1958.

The road to the presidency

1969

APRIL: Mandela writes to government calling for his own release and that of his comrades or their recognition as political prisoners. Drafts a letter to government pointing to the lenient treatment of Boer rebels and Nazi sympathizing Afrikaners during the Second World War. Government ignores his missive.

1973

DECEMBER: First visit of a cabinet minister to Robben Island: Minister of Police Jimmy Kruger meets with Nelson Mandela and a group from the single cells led by Mac Maharaj. Maharaj says Kruger had come 'on a kite-flying mission to find out whether there was scope among the political prisoners for a negotiating base with separate development as the underlying principle'. Kruger is turned down flat.

1980

OCTOBER 1: Mandela brings Supreme Court application to prevent prison warders from listening in to conversations between prisoners and their lawyers (lawyers such as Dullah Omar were essential conduits of information between Mandela and the ANC in exile). Mandela wants a decision reversed that two documents, written for his Cape Town lawyer Stanley Kawalsky, be handed to prison authorities. Judge President HEP Watermeyer and Justice EM Groskopf reserve judgement.

1981

Ronald Reagan elected president in the USA and begins 'constructive engagement toward SA'.
DECEMBER: SA forces kill more than 40 SA exiles and Lesotho nationals in Maseru, Lesotho. The target of their attack is Chris Hani, Umkhonto we Sizwe leader. Hani escapes.

1982

President PW Botha meets Zambian president Kenneth Kaunda and hosts second conference with business at the Carlton Hotel in Johannesburg to present a reform strategy. He adopts the rallying call: 'Adapt or die.'

MARCH: Government introduces the Prisons Amendment Bill which allows for remission of sentences for different categories of prisoners. Justice Minister Kobie Coetsee says government is prepared to consider releasing political prisoners.
APRIL: Mandela, Walter Sisulu, Ahmed Kathrada, Raymond Mhlaba and Andrew Mlangeni moved from Robben Island to Pollsmoor prison.
JULY: Government releases seven political prisoners – none with more than a month left to serve.

1983

Minister of Prisons Louis le Grange visits Nelson Mandela and appoints prison chief Brigadier Aucamp to act as a go-between between him and Pretoria. The Prison Board begins calling prisoners before them to discuss political issues. Mandela issues a directive to prisoners to discuss only prison-related issues and to say: 'Send your political representatives to talk with our political representatives, don't talk to me.'
MAY: ANC detonates a car bomb outside airforce headquarters in Pretoria killing 19 and injuring 215.
AUGUST: United Democratic Front is launched, embracing 700 anti-apartheid organizations.
SEPTEMBER 3: Riots break out in Sharpeville near Johannesburg as new tricameral constitution comes into effect allowing Indian and coloured people a limited say in government. Blacks are excluded.

1984

MARCH: Over 4,000 celebrities sign a petition calling for Mandela's release.
MAY: For the first time Mandela is allowed to have a contact visit with Winnie, who talks of the unbearable intimacy of touching her husband's hand for the first time in 21 years.
JUNE: Foreign Minister Pik Botha and Defence Minister Magnus Malan meet officials of Angola's government in Lusaka and demand closure of ANC camps (many camps were already heavily infiltrated with South African agents, who poisoned water or assassinated key figures, causing intense paranoia in ANC circles).
SEPTEMBER: Complaints about Nelson Mandela's incarceration at Pollsmoor, heard before a United Nations Human Rights Commission, say Mandela is sharing a damp cell with five others making it difficult for him to study.
NOVEMBER: Mandela separated from other prisoners. Mandela recalls, 'I thought I should approach the government and ask for a meeting between government and the ANC – because we are products of a collective leadership ... . The government appointed a top level team of negotiators: General Willemse, Kobie Coetsee, Niel Barnard, then head of the National Intelligence Service (NIS), constitutional expert Fanie van der Merwe and Mike Louw of NIS.' General Willemse, who became Commissioner of Prisons in 1983, and who had known Mandela since 1971 while he was commanding officer on Robben Island, said meetings took place at Pollsmoor in VIP guest houses, in the VIP dining room, in the clubhouse, once even in General Willemse's home within Pollsmoor precincts. Other meetings occurred at the home of Kobie Coetsee (he and Mandela once even played tennis) and at Victor Verster.

1985

JULY 20: State of Emergency in 36 black cities and towns; 1,000 people detained in first week.
AUGUST 15: Botha's disastrous Rubicon speech – government had promised reform would be high on the agenda, and instead Botha delivers a belligerent, blustering apologia for apartheid. The SA currency begins dropping dramatically. Academics, Afrikaans newspaper editors and businesspeople begin meeting with ANC.
OCTOBER: Harry Oppenheimer, SA's wealthiest man, publicly says he supports the release of Nelson Mandela.
NOVEMBER 21: The ANC presents their conditions for negotiations, the Harare Declaration. It demands the release of Mandela and other political prisoners, the lifting of the state of emergency, the withdrawal of troops and repressive machinery from townships, the unbanning of the ANC and the creation of conditions for free political activity. Deputy Minister of Information Louis Nel denies that this means government is considering having talks with the ANC, calling such rumours 'propaganda from behind the Iron Curtain'.
DECEMBER: Jay Naidoo, General Secretary of the newly formed Congress of SA Trade Unions, meets with ANC in Harare. Government says it will talk to the ANC if it renounces violence. The ANC says government has to renounce violence too.

1986

JANUARY: Government hints that Mandela will be released in return for the release of jailed Soviet dissidents Anatoly Shcharansky and Andrei Sakharov in Russia. This forms part of a top secret National State Security Council discussion document which discusses a range of ways to release Mandela, including releasing him outside SA, into Transkei, into a luxury villa on Robben Island, or freedom 'in exchange for something else'. It also discusses what to do if he is freed and mentions that Mandela could be given an untraceable substance that could cause his brain cells to deteriorate. The man who would head such work, Dr Wouter Basson, head of the chemical and biological warfare programme, is also personal physician to President PW Botha. In the 8 January ANC policy statement, ANC president Oliver Tambo incorporates a veiled message to Mandela: 'Our strength lies in our unity. We must guard that unity like the apple of our eye'. The ANC calls for a grand alliance against apartheid incorporating businessmen, whites and opinion makers to force government to the negotiating table by 1990.
FEBRUARY: In his opening of parliament address Botha says apartheid is outdated and commits his administration to moving away from it.
MARCH 16: Signing of the Nkomati Accord with Samora Machel, president of Mozambique, which pledges to have ANC removed from Mozambican soil. Botha says: 'We cannot escape the fact that peace too has its price'.
MARCH: Talks between Congress of SA Trade Unions (Cosatu) leaders

Jay Naidoo, Sydney Mafumadi and Cyril Ramaphosa, in Harare with ANC. Cosatu had become a key conduit in the traffic of information between Mandela and ANC in exile.
MAY: Commonwealth Eminent Persons Group gives government a proposal with a deadline: release Mandela, unban the ANC, declare a truce with the ANC, and begin negotiations. Government rejects this. In part government is rattled by growing far right-wing militancy – a National Party rally had been broken up by the Afrikaner Weerstandsbeweging (Afrikaner Resistance Movement) in Pietersburg. Divisions in the ruling government cabinet are becoming apparent. It is publicly known that Kobie Coetsee had seen Mandela at least once and was impressed by him.
OCTOBER: Samora Machel's aircraft crashes within SA killing him and 38 others; ongoing claims that SA agents caused the crash.
NOVEMBER: Ahmed Kathrada writes to Helen Joseph that they had been allowed to visit Mandela four times since his operation in March that year.

1987
JANUARY 8: ANC slogan 'Our goal is in sight'.
JULY: Institute for Democratic Alternative directors Alex Boraine and Frederick van Zyl Slabbert lead a large group of businesspeople, academics, writers and poets to Dakar, Senegal, for talks with ANC leaders. The ANC moots two-sided negotiations with the government and its partners on one side and the allied 'forces of freedom' on the other.
AUGUST 13: President PW Botha instructs Justice Minister Kobie Coetsee to prepare the release of ANC Rivonia trialist Govan Mbeki (77). Botha says decisions to release jailed ANC leaders will no longer depend on whether they renounced violence.
OCTOBER: Mbeki, released after 24 years in prison, cannot be quoted, nor allowed outside Port Elizabeth.

1988
JANUARY 8: ANC slogan 'Plan, organize, attack. United action for people's power'.
APRIL 15: National Party MPs Albert Nothnagel and Con Botha tell parliament that all political groups including the ANC will have to be included in negotiations.
MAY: After two years' work, the ANC releases a draft constitution for SA. There is increasing unhappiness among top National Party leaders with Botha's bombastic ways.
DECEMBER: Mandela is transferred to Victor Verster prison in Paarl, where private meetings with government representatives can be held.

1989
JANUARY 8: ANC statement, 'Regime is not softening in any way'.
JANUARY 18: PW Botha (73) suffers a mild stroke; attended by Dr Basson.
FEBRUARY 2: Botha resigns as party leader; FW de Klerk elected. De Klerk builds closer ties with moderate black leaders (Mangosuthu Buthelezi, Inkatha Freedom Party, and Alan Hendrickse, Labour Party).
MAY: Botha announces 6 September elections.
JULY 5: Botha meets Mandela at Tuynhuys, Cape Town. Botha forced to resign by his cabinet.
SEPTEMBER: FW de Klerk voted into power.
OCTOBER 15: All remaining Rivonia Trialists except Mandela released. Leaders of Mass Democratic Movement in busy shuttle of information between Mandela and ANC.

1990
JANUARY 8: ANC statement, 'Year of People's Action for a democratic SA'.
JANUARY 17: Department of Justice says it is reviewing restrictions on all banned organizations including the ANC and SA Communist Party.
FEBRUARY 2: De Klerk announces unbanning of all restricted political organizations.
FEBRUARY 11: Mandela released.
APRIL: First four ANC negotiators arrive; Matthews Phosa and Jacob Zuma lead initial ANC negotiations.
MAY 2–4: Government and ANC meet formally for the first time and hammer out Groote Schuur Minute.
AUGUST 6: First agreement, the Pretoria Minute, on indemnity and return home of ANC exiles and the release of political prisoners, reached. ANC leaders from exile given year-long renewable permits to remain in SA.

1991
JANUARY 29: Mandela and Buthelezi discuss ways to find peace in KwaZulu-Natal; accord quickly disintegrates.

APRIL 3: Mandela, addressing US Congress members and their aides behind closed doors in Cape Town, delivers a tirade against De Klerk about the continuing violence.
APRIL 4: Mandela tells the ANC National Executive Committee meeting that he was wrong to call De Klerk a 'man of integrity'.
APRIL 5: ANC delivers a publicized ultimatum to De Klerk giving him until 9 May to take seven steps to end violence or talks will cease.
JULY 19: Inkathagate scandal breaks: the government had helped fund Inkatha including money for rallies held in November 1989 and March 1989. Allegations are rife that it is supplying Inkatha with guns and giving military training to its cadres.
SEPTEMBER 14: National Peace Conference held in Johannesburg, first face-to-face meeting of Mandela, De Klerk and Buthelezi on one platform, their unhappy faces in photographs display the mood – and portents for success of the meeting.
NOVEMBER 28–29: Sixty delegates from 20 parties hold talks at the Holiday Inn near Johannesburg International Airport to lay the ground rules for multiparty talks. The Pan-Africanist Congress walks out on the second day.
DECEMBER 20–21: The Convention for a Democratic SA (Codesa) begins with 18 delegations and government. Chief Buthelezi refuses to attend but sends delegates. De Klerk delivers a broadside against the ANC, and a furious Mandela lashes back.

1992
MARCH 17: After a major defeat in a by-election in Potchefstroom for the National Party, De Klerk calls for a referendum on his policies; 68,6% of the all-white voters show their support of negotiations.
MAY 15–16: Codesa holds its second plenary session. Muted progress.
JUNE 17: Boipatong massacre; 46 people killed by Inkatha *impi* from KwaMadala hostel. The ANC withdraws from talks.
SEPTEMBER 7: Ill-considered ANC/SACP march on Bisho, capital of Ciskei. Troops open fire and 29 die and 200 injured.
SEPTEMBER 26: Mandela and De Klerk sign a Record of Understanding to get negotiations back on the table – and to curb violence.
NOVEMBER 16: Judge Richard Goldstone announces his commis-

sion (investigating misconduct in the police and military) has conducted a raid on Military Intelligence's covert operations centre uncovering files of data about state involvement in assassinations and covert fomenting of violence. De Klerk appoints the Steyn Commission which a month later suspends or retires 23 officers in what is felt is a facile damage control exercise.

1993
FEBRUARY 12: ANC and government announce agreement in principle on a five-year transition during which a government of national unity, formed by the main election winners, will govern.
MARCH 5–6: Codesa resumes in earnest after 10-month break as delegates race toward a 1994 election, overcoming numerous obstacles, particularly those imposed by right-wing violence such as bombings and killings.
APRIL 1–2: Codesa holds its third plenary session with 25 parties participating, including the white right-wing Conservative Party.
APRIL 10: Assassination of Chris Hani by a right-wing assassin.
APRIL 24: Oliver Tambo, president of the ANC from 1967 to 1991, dies of a stroke aged 75.

1994
APRIL 26: First democratic elections for all races. First day of elections for pregnant women and the elderly, open to general public from the next day and continuing for five days, with a further day in KwaZulu-Natal because of logistical problems.
MAY 10: Nelson Mandela is inaugurated President with Thabo Mbeki and FW de Klerk as his deputies.

1999
JUNE 2: South Africa's second democratic election is held. African National Congress president Thabo Mbeki is elected president of South Africa.

The first steps

We are not yet free, we have merely achieved the
freedom to be free, the right not to be oppressed.
We have not taken the final step on our journey, but
the first step on a longer and even more difficult
road. For to be free is not merely to cast off
one's chains, but to live in a way that respects
and enhances the freedom of others.

NELSON MANDELA
LONG WALK TO FREEDOM, 1994

There are many places to begin the story of Nelson Rolihlahla Mandela. It could start at his birth, on 18 July 1918 in the small village of Mvezo in Transkei of the Eastern Cape, one of the most beautiful and isolated regions of South Africa. Although he was born of royal Thembu blood, the Great Place of the Thembu where he was raised by his uncle King Jongintaba is, even today, a modest compound: a cluster of homes and a single modern house enfolded by steep mountains. In winter the hills are ablaze with vivid red hot pokers. In summer the valleys are lush and green, and pink and purple cosmos cluster at roadsides. The Great Place is more humble than the home Mandela built in nearby Qunu after his release from 27 years in jail, a house that is a replica of the one in which he spent his last years of incarceration at Victor Verster prison in Paarl.

Mandela's story could begin at his birth, but it may be apt to begin at the start of the colonization of Africa, to understand the passions aroused by those subjugated by colonial forces. As VV Mudimbe wrote: 'The past is with us, not behind us. The traditions from which we come are in our words each and every day.'

The youthful Mandela was an imperious man and a talented boxer and lawyer. He rose through the ranks of the African National Congress Youth League in the early 1940s, pushing to the front of resistance marches and, two decades later, battling to make effective bombs for the armed wing of the African National Congress (ANC), Umkhonto we Sizwe (MK), which he formed and led.

While always an impressive leader, he was but one of many exceptional black men and women who emerged and began discarding the chains of racism. It was not necessarily apparent in the 1940s, 50s or even 60s that Mandela would become the man of greatness he did. Certainly he was legendary in the 1950s and 1960s but, as anyone who lived through the resistance struggles of South Africa will tell you, there were many who became legendary because of their leadership, bravery or compassion, and either died at the hands of the apartheid state, or were left behind by the course of events and subsided into relative obscurity and, for some, sad and lonely deaths in poverty.

A young student teacher, who saw Mandela adjudicating a debate between the Jan Hofmeyr School of Social Work and the Bantu Natural College in Johannesburg in 1951, later commented: 'There was nothing striking about him, he was very judicial and very precise,

PAGES 14 AND 15: In 1952 Nelson Mandela and Oliver Tambo established the first black law practice in Johannesburg.

OPPOSITE: Mandela wearing a beaded Thembu collar.

LEFT: Mandela was a keen amateur boxer in his youth.

careful in making judgements, he tried to make allowances.' Ten years later this teacher, Desmond Tutu, became a priest of the Anglican Church, and over the years one of the most beloved men in South Africa. In 1984 he was awarded a Nobel Peace Prize, which has been conferred on three other South Africans; two were leaders of the ANC, Mandela himself shared the prize in 1993 with former State President, Frederick Willem de Klerk, and ANC president Albert Luthuli in 1960.

An early member of Umkhonto we Sizwe recalls that, when Nelson Mandela visited London in 1961 and addressed a '... deep underground cell meeting to give us a briefing of what was happening in the country, he was confident, but we were not certain that his information was up to standard. It aroused some debate at the time'.

Ben Turok, an ANC parliamentarian who has been politically active since the 1940s, says: 'From the mid-80s Mandela became a symbol, but not because of his great leadership. The movement built him up. The movement decided "There's this guy, let's focus around him." We had no contact with him. [ANC president, Oliver] Tambo had a bit of contact for a long time. The movement decided it needed a symbol; Mandela was the ideal hero of the struggle. It was decided: put him in the front line, campaign across the world for his release.' In terms of contemporary history, this statement may seem

Albert Luthuli, president of the African National Congress from 1952 to 1961 and 1960 Nobel Peace Prize winner, outside his house in Groutville, KwaZulu-Natal.

remarkable, but a look at ANC documents of the 1980s shows he may in fact be right. And in the end the prayers of a nation were more than answered when Nelson Mandela proved to be not only a suitable leader, but one of the most remarkable men the world has known.

The South African concept of *ubuntu* (a person is only a person because of other people) is most powerfully felt in the leadership of a competent politician, and without doubt in the tremendous humanity of Nelson Mandela. His story is in many ways more than that of just one person; without the exceptional courage of humble folk, who risk their lives and for whom no amount of bannings or persecution can end a desire for freedom and justice, no leaders can emerge to carry a cause forward.

No other twentieth century leader, except Mahatma Gandhi, whose life was also forged by South African racism and paternalism, has aroused such adoration from his people as Nelson Mandela. Only he and Gandhi have been able to unite bitter foes by setting personal examples of their own humility and efforts to reconcile a nation torn apart by bigotry and fear.

Although both saw reconciliation and negotiation as the way to heal their nations, neither was ever prepared to be cowed. Gandhi wrote that *satya* (love) and *agraha* (firmness) '... engenders and serves as a synonym for force ... *satyagraha* is not passive resistance'.

Indeed, Gandhi wrote that it was '... cowardice to bend one's knee before an oppressor'. These beliefs had a powerful impact on Mandela and the ANC of the 1940s and 50s. However, while *satyagraha* may have been effective against a government that had a conscience, such as the British Empire, and could be moved by the suffering of those who protested injustice, it was ineffective against the barbarity of apartheid's governors, and thus Mandela and his followers turned to armed resistance in 1961.

While Germany, a shattered and humiliated nation after the Second World War, had the Marshall Plan to cling to, Nelson Mandela has given South Africans important lessons in humility and compassion. He has bestowed a sense of nationhood on a country deeply and deliberately divided. For the first time, South Africa's motto (Unity is Strength), adopted when it became a republic in 1961, finally means something. While Mandela's greatness has been all-encompassing, it has been the little ways in which he demonstrated humanity that have touched a world starved of moral guidance. Land Affairs and Agriculture Minister Derek Hanekom says, 'Mandela is not always humble in private, but in public he has a way of approaching people and making them feel special. One of my staff wanted to meet him, and when she shook his hand she told him her cousin was a well-known sports personality.

South Africa was instrumental in forming the passionate resistance to racism and colonialism of Mahatma Gandhi (centre).

Mandela said to her: "Well, I will never again wash my hand, I am so honoured to have shaken yours". It meant so much to her.' Not long after the Ambassador for the United States James Joseph arrived in South Africa and, before his credentials had been presented, he was at an event with his wife. They wanted a photograph with the President but were loath to intrude. Mandela, catching sight of them out of the corner of his eye, walked up to them. 'He held his hand out and said, "I would be most honoured if you would let me have my photograph taken with you",' Joseph remembers.

Dr Uwe Kaestner, ambassador of the Federal Republic of Germany recalls Mandela's state visit to Germany in May 1996, when he addressed the German *Bundestag* (parliament): 'After his speech, that was received with a standing ovation, he did not return to his seat but went straight to the Leader of the Christian Democratic Party caucus, Dr Wolfgang Schauble, who as a result of an assassination attempt is wheelchairbound. Mandela spontaneously greeted and embraced Dr Schauble – in a gesture that certainly was not in any protocol programme.' The capacity to empathize is one of Mandela's greatest attributes.

The South African constitution notes that South Africa is united in its diversity. But it does not note one area where many are united: in our love for Nelson Mandela. This book tells the story of a country's quest to be free, and of Nelson Mandela, just a man, a person because of other persons, and the greatest of all South Africans.

REPRESSION AND RESISTANCE

The men who formed the South African Native National Congress (later the ANC) in Bloemfontein were men of deep thought. They sat at their desks in publishing houses and discussed the plight of South Africa's Africans, and what Jefferson, Descartes or Rousseau would have made of it. They sat on rolled-up overcoats in verdant valleys, blankets around their shoulders, and passed pipes filled with pungent tobacco, musing on how the 100-year wars of dispossession of the nineteenth century continued into the new century. They sat on cold concrete bunks with tin braziers spitting sparks of light into cold migrant workers' hostels, as they talked of the lands from which they had been forced, and the mines where they had to toil, and ways in which the black man could regain his country, his pride and his birthright.

So, in 1912, they came to Bloemfontein by train and on bicycles, ox carts and foot to found the Native National Congress, two years after the Union of South Africa was formed and one year before the government instituted a process which led to the radical removal of land rights from African people. White colonists were unhappy with any African ownership of land. Through wars, and later laws, of dispossession, they pushed African peoples into smaller and smaller rural areas, and introduced taxes to force them to seek work in the growing urban areas and mines.

These issues troubled the intellectuals of the Native National Congress, who attempted a discourse with government and opposition parties while building support among unionized workers. However, after the 1922 mineworkers' strike, when the red flag of socialism began waving at more rallies, the National Party government of General Albert Hertzog intervened to advantage white workers. The burgeoning multiracial union movement began disintegrating and black unionism started to rise. White workers started a long process of disinterest in labour as successive governments progressively clamped down on black unions. These included, over the years, particularly under apartheid from 1948, certain categories of reserved jobs for whites, and a prohibition on black people from rising to any post where they might be in a position of authority over white workers.

RIGHT: The African National Congress of the 1930s was led by the man whose vision saw it founded, Pixley kaIsaka Seme. However, in the 1930s the group of intellectuals that led it failed to inspire and saw the ANC struggle to survive.

Govan Mbeki, who was later jailed with Mandela, wrote: 'The decade 1936 to 1946 marked a departure from years of inactivity to a new phase in the struggle for liberation. The All-African Convention [AAC] had been convened for the specific purpose of marshalling Africans in every walk of life to fight the disenfranchisement of African voters in the Cape. But with the passing of the Representation of Natives Act in 1936 the AAC failed in its task.' This law placed black voters in the Cape, the only place where they had been able to vote during the past 80 years, on a separate voters' roll.

Mandela considered this situation carefully when he joined the African National Congress Youth League in 1944 under the leadership of Anton Lembede. Mandela and his friends Oliver Tambo and Walter Sisulu rapidly rose to senior positions. They had already noted a pattern emerging between the State and its black subjects that would embed itself in South African political life: repression, resistance, severe repression, followed by stronger resistance which would over the years see those opposed to apartheid be increasingly driven underground and into more militant subterfuge.

During my lifetime I have dedicated myself to this struggle of the African people. I have fought against white domination, and I have fought against black domination. I have cherished the ideal of a democratic and free society in which all persons live together in harmony and with equal opportunities. It is an ideal which I hope to live for and achieve. But if needs be, it is an ideal for which I am prepared to die.

NELSON MANDELA
DURING HIS TRIAL IN 1963

People collecting signatures on 24 June 1955 for the adoption of the Freedom Charter. On 26 June the Congress of the People drew up the Freedom Charter at Kliptown, a village near Johannesburg.

THE M PLAN

In 1950 began a string of annual events centring around 26 June: the African National Congress and South African Indian Congress declared a National Day of Protest and Mourning in the wake of 1949 riots between Africans and Indians in Natal. Influenced by the non-violent protest actions advocated by Mahatma Gandhi (*see* page 18), on 26 June 1952 the Campaign for the Defiance of Unjust Laws was launched by the ANC and the South African Indian Congress, and 8,400 volunteers went to jail for defying apartheid legislation. Mandela was volunteer in chief and Yusuf Cachalia his deputy. The Transvaal Law Society immediately tried to have the sign 'Mandela and Tambo', on the second floor window of Chancellor House near the Johannesburg Magistrates' Courts, removed. Mandela and Tambo had only months before begun their law practice. The Society petitioned the Supreme Court to have Mandela struck off the attorneys' roll because of his role in the Defiance Campaign. They failed.

OPPOSITE: Dr JS Moroka, Nelson Mandela and Yusuf Dadoo during the 1952 Defiance Campaign.

BELOW: Yusuf Dadoo, one of the most important Indian leaders of the South African resistance struggle, and Nelson Mandela surrender to the police during the Defiance Campaign.

THIS PAGE, CLOCKWISE FROM RIGHT *(Treason Trial): Helen Joseph, one of the 156 Treason Trialists. Mandela leaves the Old Synagogue, Pretoria, 1958, with Moses Kotane. Mandela sings with supporters after his acquittal. Mandela arrives at the Old Drill Hall, Johannesburg, 1956.*

OPPOSITE: *Mandela stands out among his fellow accused in the centre of the third row.*

TREASON TRIAL

The ACCUSED

DECEMBER 1956

Mandela, realizing the increasing need for secrecy, devised the M Plan. Govan Mbeki reflects, 'The government, by its repressive laws, kept pushing us deeper and deeper underground, honing our recruitment and actions, making us better and better.' The M Plan saw branches of the ANC divided into cells based on a single street; seven cells would make a zone and four zones comprised one ward. Later forming the basis of the ANC's underground cell structure for political activists and Umkhonto we Sizwe, the M Plan was successfully used in the 1980s (though it was not known by this name at this stage) as street committees and block committees sprang up in every township to resist apartheid.

The M plan was an essential element of all that was to follow. In 1953, Professor ZK Matthews, one of the ANC's most respected leaders, influenced by the Atlantic Charter and Roosevelt's Four Freedoms (freedom of speech and expression, freedom of worship, freedom from want and freedom from fear), suggested a Freedom Charter. That year, the National Conference of the ANC called for the organization of a Congress of the People. Convened at Kliptown, near Johannesburg, on 26 June 1955, the Congress drew up the Freedom Charter – a declaration of basic principles – that would become the ANC's seminal organizational and policy manifesto for almost four decades.

The Treason Trial began in 1956 and continued for four years. Among the 156 accused were Oliver Tambo, Nelson Mandela, Walter Sisulu, Ben Turok (who had written the economic clause of the Charter) and Helen Joseph. During the trial the State tried, and failed, to prove the Freedom Charter was a Communist document. Towards the end of March 1961, Mandela appeared at the All-In Conference in Pietermaritzburg and called for a national convention before South Africa became a republic – releasing it from its imperial ties with Britain.

Mandela and the ANC organized a general strike for 29 to 31 May during which 10,000 people, mostly African, refused to go to work, but a massive police clampdown saw the strike faltering on the second day. Mandela devoted five pages of a 13-page report on the strike to lashing the press for its cowardice in reporting accurately on the build-up to the strike, and later publishing articles saying the strike had failed.

New Age was the most important newspaper of the 1950s for those who were opposed to apartheid.

In its letter 'Freedom Justice and Dignity', released on 26 June 1961 from underground headquarters, the ANC said: 'A full scale and countrywide campaign of non-cooperation with the government will be launched immediately ... we plan to make government impossible. Those who are voteless cannot be expected to continue paying taxes to a government which is not responsible to them... .' In January 1962 Mandela travelled to North and East Africa where he met major African leaders, underwent military training with the Algerian army and briefly met Umkhonto we Sizwe members who had left the country in order to set up military units abroad.

Not long after his return to South Africa he was arrested and charged with leaving the country illegally and inciting workers to strike. He appeared in court with an animal hide draped across his shoulders; his wife Winnie wore traditional Xhosa dress. In his statement from the dock in 1962, after which he was sentenced to three years in prison, he said: 'The ANC's policy was one which appealed to my deepest inner convictions. It sought for the unity of all Africans, overriding tribal differences among them. It sought the acquisition of political power for Africans in the land of their birth. ... I have always regarded myself in the first instance as an African patriot. ... Today I am attracted by the idea of a classless society.' The speeches were perhaps overly dramatic for the relative insignificance of the charges, but Mandela was speaking to history.

general strike by NELSON MANDELA
(Secretary, National Action Council of South Africa)

A REPORT OF THE 3-DAY STRIKE IN SOUTH AFRICA (MAY 29, 30, 31, 1961)

ABOVE: *A police clampdown saw the 1961 general strike fail, as documented in this 13-page report by Nelson Mandela.*

LEFT: *Mandela in 1962 at the Algerian military headquarters where he received training while he was underground. During this period he was known as the 'Black Pimpernel'.*

In 1962 Nelson Mandela left South Africa and visited other African countries. He also met political leaders in London. Here he is photographed outside Westminster Abbey.

Golden Rules for a Good Congress Member. Lead – don't Order! Congress members must be close to the people and trusted by them. They must lead, not dictate to the people.

AFRICAN NATIONAL CONGRESS HANDBOOK, 1952 (PRICE ONE SHILLING)

The first steps

Eight of the convicted Rivonia Trialists: (top row from left) Nelson Mandela, Walter Sisulu, Govan Mbeki and Raymond Mhlaba; (bottom row from left) Elias Motsoaledi, Andrew Mlangeni, Ahmed Kathrada and Dennis Goldberg.

On 11 July 1963 history knocked – at the door of Lilliesleaf Farm in Rivonia north of Johannesburg, to be precise; for approximately two years, the movement had used this farm as a safe house. All of the members of Umkhonto we Sizwe's High Command, barring Wilton Mkwayi who would be detained later, were arrested here.

Mandela was transferred a few months after this from Robben Island, where he was serving his three-year sentence, to join his comrades in the Pretoria Local prison. He was charged in this, the Rivonia Trial (officially known as 'The State versus the National High Command and others), on 156 counts.

The accused realized that the State was seeking the death sentence for their activities. It failed in this quest and sentenced them all to life imprisonment on Robben Island (with the exception of one of the co-accused, Dennis Goldberg, who served his sentence in Pretoria Central as the political section of the Island was reserved for black prisoners).

UMKHONTO WE SIZWE

'Umkhonto we Sizwe will be at the front line of the people's defence. It will be the fighting arm of the people against the government and its policies of race oppression. It will be the striking force of the people for liberty, for rights and for their final liberation' – Manifesto of Umkhonto we Sizwe military wing of the African National Congress.

In 1961, Mandela wrote after the three-day general strike (*see also* page 28): 'Is it politically correct to continue preaching peace and non-violence when dealing with a government whose barbaric practices have brought so much suffering and misery to Africans?'

Govan Mbeki wrote: 'At a meeting of peasants during the Defiance Campaign [*see* page 25], one aged man [argued] with typical down to earth peasant logic that Africans had lost the Wars of Dispossession because the weapons they used did not match those of the Boers or the British. According to him, unless that imbalance was corrected there was no point in embarking on a defiance of unjust laws. Any talk of nonviolence in conducting such a campaign was merely to tickle the Boers ('Niyawa-nyubuza Amabhulu; Le ea oa Tsikinyetsa Ma Buru'). Having said this, he took his old military coat which he had folded to sit on, shook the grass off, and moved away.'

Whether to take up arms was a decision that took the ANC seven years to reach. Mac Maharaj, former Minister of Transport, recalls: 'As far back as 1953 he [Mandela], together with comrade Walter Sisulu, began to explore the need for and the possibilities of the armed struggle. He expressed his view at a public meeting and was summoned to explain his actions before the National Executive Committee. He accepted the reprimand of his peers and his seniors. He never saw this dressing down as a personal affront. It helped hone his instincts for reading the moment and understanding the rules by which one strove to better shape the ANC to discharge its responsibilities.'

It was a difficult decision, and one that caused heated debate within the ANC's inner circles, but it was a decision that had popular approval. Albert Camus in *Letters to a German Friend*, written in 1943, in his role as a French resistance pamphleteer during the Second World War, described the difficulty of taking such a decision. He said that the French Resistance's hesitation in making the decision to take up arms meant that '... we paid for it with humiliations and silences, with bitter experiences, with prison sentences, with executions at dawn, with desertions and separations, with daily pangs of hunger, with emaciated children and above all with humiliation of our human dignity.... It took us all that time to find out if we had the right to kill

Winnie Mandela in traditional Xhosa dress (centre) with Violet Weinberg (on the right in a checked dress) and well-wishers during the Rivonia Trial.

men... . It taught us that the spirit is of no avail against the sword, but that the spirit together with the sword will always win the day over the sword alone... .' These words could have been written by a member of the African National Congress, not only in the early 1960s, but until the day of democratic elections in 1994.

The laws which the National Party government rushed onto the Statute books within the first two years of its 1948 election victory, and the harshness which they meted out to any voices of dissent, lent weight to the argument for an armed struggle. The laws pushed through in their first years of government made race an overwhelming determiner of whom South Africans could love and where they could live and seek work; they made humiliation the daily burden of the black South African, and opportunity the exclusive preserve of white people. The laws included the Prohibition of Mixed Marriages Act (1949), The Immorality Amendment Act (1950), Population Registration Act (1950), Suppression of Communism Act (1950), The Group Areas Act (1950), Natives Abolition of Passes and Co-Ordination of Documents Act (1952), Separate Amenities Act (1953), Bantu Education Act (1953), and others that excluded black people from universities in white areas and compelled blacks, who formed 80 percent of the population, to live on 13 percent of the land – and that the least arable land in the country.

During the early days of MK its leader Mandela knew nothing of warfare, of weapons, of military strategy. A dandy lawyer, he would have to adopt military fatigues, crawl through mud and kill. The late Joe Slovo, a Johannesburg lawyer who would become MK Chief of Staff, recalled the first days in 1960 and 1961: 'Among the lot of us we did not have a single pistol. No-one we knew had ever engaged in urban sabotage with home made explosives. Jack Hodgson had been through the war, a veteran of the Abyssinian campaign and a full time leader of the [anti-fascist and anti-apartheid] Springbok Legion. Into Jack's and Rica's flat, sacks of permanganate of potash were brought and we spent days with mortars and pestles grinding this substance to a fine powder. After December 16 [1960] most homes were raided but not the Hodgsons'.' This substance, more commonly used in washing lettuce, mixed with aluminium powder and catalysed by a drop of acid could make an effective explosion. For timing devices they experimented to find out how long it took the acid to eat through various thicknesses of cardboard.

With such a primitive mechanism Slovo set out to burn down the Johannesburg Drill Hall, where the preparatory examination of the Treason Trial of 1956 was held. He entered the hall and found about 50 cleaners polishing the floors and wooden chairs. He put the bottle upside down behind a cupboard and then heard, 'Can I do anything for you, sir?' Slovo, knowing there were a scant 15 minutes before the acid dripped through the potash and exploded, said his brother had received call-up papers but needed to take an exam. The officer asked Slovo to follow him. Fortunately the exemptions officer was not there, and Slovo was asked to come back another day. As soon as he could, he grabbed the tennis ball cylinder which housed the ingredients and defused the bomb.

He and his friends discovered the next day that Petros Molefe had been killed near his target by a premature explosion, the first MK cadre to die in action. The first test explosions of MK bombs took place at a disused brickworks. Mandela led this expedition which launched Molotov cocktails against a wall. The next test involved placing a bomb in a pit. According to their calculations the bomb should have exploded in 15 minutes. When, after 25 minutes it had still not exploded, a volunteer climbed into the pit and adjusted the bomb.

OPPOSITE: Yusuf Dadoo and Joe Slovo demonstrate in London for the Rivonia Trialists to be spared the noose.

In 1979 the ANC's highly disciplined Solomon Mahlangu Unit targeted the oil refineries of Sasol One and Sasol Two. These operations were among the most significant ANC military victories and saw no loss of life. This unit also hit several oil storage depots like the one depicted here.

He was barely out of the pit when there was a huge explosion. A number of blasts took place not long after that. In 1961, Joe Gqabi and Joe Modise, leading a unit to New Canada rail station at 3 a.m., took a stone, tied it to a wire and threw it across the line supplying the electricity. Modise recalled: 'We saw a blue flame coming out of the electric wire when the contact was made. We were sure there was going to be a short circuit but to our disappointment an hour later a train passed. Joe Gqabi then placed a stick of dynamite on the line and although it exploded the damage was minimal.' They later went to Mondeor, a Johannesburg suburb, almost rural in those days and sparsely populated, and destroyed telephone lines by tying a wire to the lines and pulling them down with the car. Ebrahim Ismail Ebrahim was part of the Natal high command along with Ronnie Kasrils, Billy Nair and Curnick Ndlovu (Bruno Mtolo, Mr X in the Rivonia Trial, who betrayed his former friends, was also a member). Ebrahim recalled his early training as '… crude, we only had dynamite which we stole; we had no revolvers or AKs, let alone knew how to use them'. The first time they stole dynamite they found little pieces with the explosive which they threw away, only to learn later that these were the detonators.

Oliver Tambo, Commander in Chief of Umkhonto we Sizwe (MK), said at the twenty-fifth anniversary of the organization in 1986, a time when detentions and repression were at their highest in South Africa: 'Our problem was not whether to fight but how to continue the fight. We of the ANC had always stood for a non-racial democracy and we shrank from any action which might drive the races further apart than they already were. But fifty years of non-violence [before the formation of MK] had brought the African people nothing but more and more repressive legislation and fewer and fewer rights.'

Essentially MK remained a ragtag army, poorly resourced with increasing tendencies in the 1980s toward torture and repression of rogue elements, or those who were suspected by officials of being spies in its camps. The June 1976 uprising of Soweto youth against the Afrikaans language as a medium of instruction, largely motivated by the Black Consciousness Movement, transformed the thin guerrilla army. Thousands of young people left South Africa after police opened fire on marching pupils, killing 10-year-old Hector Petersen and many others.

A firestorm whipped around the country carrying talk of revolution and the beginning of the end of white rule.

The twenty-fifth anniversary issue of the MK journal *Dawn* noted: 'Almost overnight the Soweto generation enabled us to breach the barriers by which the enemy had sought to separate us from the masses.' Thousands of young people streamed across the borders to begin military training for the ANC and the Pan-Africanist Congress, which was opposed to white participation in the liberation struggle and even less prepared than MK. Highly motivated, bright and angry, they would change the lives of all they encountered – including their own. They entered an organization that was ill-prepared for such a huge influx.

By the time the ANC held its National Consultative Conference in Lusaka in 1985 (26 years after the last legal conference in South Africa) it was clear that the armed struggle was still seen by the ANC as the primary means of struggle: '... our armed units should be based among the masses of our people, relying on them for protection and sustenance, and, at the same time, drawing greater and greater numbers of our people into combat'.

Electricity pylons were one of the first targets of the ANC's armed wing Umkhonto we Sizwe.

Love never gives up

*I may be able to speak the languages
of men and even of angels, but if I have
no love, my speech is no more than a
noisy gong or a clanging bell. I may
have the gift of inspired preaching ...
but if I have no love I am nothing.
I may give away everything I have
and even give up my body to be burnt
– but if I have no love, this does me no
good. Love is patient and kind; it is
not jealous or conceited or proud;
love is not ill-mannered or selfish or
irritable; love does not keep a record
of wrongs; love is not happy with evil,
but is happy with the truth. Love
never gives up; and its faith, hope
and patience never fail.*

CORINTHIANS 13
READ BY ARCHBISHOP DESMOND TUTU AT THE
MARRIAGE OF NELSON MANDELA AND GRAÇA MACHEL,
18 JULY 1998

Even an 80-year-old man has to consult his chief about his marriage, even in modern times. So it was that President Nelson Mandela, a fortnight after he married Samora Machel's widow Graça, travelled to the former homeland of Transkei, where he grew up, to ask forgiveness from the Thembu elders for not seeking their approval. Some had voiced anger that he had not consulted them, but not all shared this disquiet. Congress of Traditional Leaders president Patekile Holomisa said Mandela's marriage on his eightieth birthday, on 18 July 1998, revived an ancient practice: 'Sons of our chiefs used to marry daughters of other tribes. That brought peace between the tribes and consolidated their relations. So Mandela has symbolically strengthened relations between South Africa and Mozambique.'

Paramount chief Buyilikwayo Dalindyebo, king of the Thembu and the son of Mandela's nephew, the revered Sabata Dalindyebo, is four decades Mandela's junior. He also had no qualms about Mandela's not sticking to the letter of custom. A modern king, he balances tradition with the norms and strictures of modernity. For example, he has only one wife, although tradition allows him more: Mandela's father, Gadla Henry Mphakanyiswa, was a senior chief with four wives, Mandela's beloved mother, Nosekeni Fanny, being his third.

Stemming from Mandela's love for his mother (a visit to her grave was one of his first tasks on leaving prison) is an abiding regard for all women. In a crowded room, he gravitates toward women, shaking their hands, hugging those he knows and asking after details one would not expect a man who meets so many to recall. Sensitive to the hardships suffered particularly by rural women, he has paid special attention to women's rights – a third of the ANC's parliamentary posts are reserved for women. Recognizing that, without affirmation of women, men will pay only lip service to their advancement, Mandela has taken businesspeople to Qunu to enlist their help in developing the region. So far few have given more than promises.

When his uncle Chief Jongintaba Dalindyebo tried to arrange a marriage for him in 1940, the 22-year-old Mandela fled to Johannesburg, not feeling ready for such a commitment. He knew that he had a destiny broader than the hills of Transkei could contain. When he met women he sought the sweetness of his mother and a person with a strong sense of herself as an individual. He lost interest in one woman because she lacked this quality.

Mandela, who wanted to be a lawyer, had done some studies toward a Bachelor of Arts degree at Fort Hare University. There he met and became friends with Oliver Tambo, a fellow member of the Bible Society who shared his legal ambitions. Tambo led the ANC into exile in 1960 and helped ensure its continuation and growth despite the odds.

PAGES 38 AND 39: Nelson Mandela and Graça Machel in Pretoria at the wedding of Jeff Radebe, Minister of Public Works.

BELOW: A house at the Great Place of the Thembu, Eastern Cape, where Nelson Mandela lived as a boy.

Nelson Mandela and his first wife Evelyn Ntoko Mase, from whom he was estranged in 1953. The couple had four children together: Maki, Makgatho and Thembi (their first daughter died at nine months and their second daughter was given the same name, Maki).

But, when Mandela and Tambo met in the early 1940s, they could not guess at what lay 20 years ahead. In 1940 Mandela, fleeing the marriage his uncle planned, moved to Johannesburg, where he met a quiet, pretty girl four years his junior. Evelyn Ntoko Mase was a nurse with the Chamber of Mines and the daughter of a Transkei mineworker. A few months later they married in a quiet ceremony, but she was ultimately not suited to a man with the political ambitions of Mandela. In 1953 Mandela and Evelyn were estranged. Despite the intervention of Mandela's cousin, Kaizer Matanzima, the marriage could not be salvaged. Mandela made it clear to Evelyn that no attempt to save the nine-year marriage was worth the trouble, and the divorce came through in 1958. On moving out of their Orlando West home Evelyn took their children Maki (2), Makgatho (5) and Thembi (8). She returned to Transkei where she opened a general dealer's store. Thembi died in a car accident in 1969 while Mandela was in jail, but he was not allowed to attend the funeral. Evelyn, a devout Jehovah's Witness, today lives in a comfortable home in rural Cofimvaba, the living room filled with photographs of her grandchildren. She has no bitterness about her divorce, and says their marriage broke up because, 'Mandela wanted me to join politics and I wanted him to follow God.'

In 1955, Mandela met a 23-year-old girl with flawless skin, a ready laugh and passions as strong as his. Winnie Nomzamo Madikizela seemed the perfect match for him, awakening in him a deep, romantic love. The daughter of Columbus Madikizela, a prominent Transkei politician, she came from an important family, and was perhaps better suited to him than Evelyn, whose origins were humble. Winnie was the first black social work student at Baragwanath Hospital. Here, at last, Nelson had found a woman passionate about politics and her individuality. He found in Winnie a ready listener for his political views. She was astute in her judgements and ready to respond to a political call to action. Winnie recalls that just over two years later he pulled up in his car and said, 'There is this woman, a dressmaker, you must go and see her, she is going to make your wedding gown. How many bridesmaids would you like?' They married on 14 June 1958. Zenani was born in February the next year and Zindzi followed in December 1960. Winnie immersed herself in motherhood and political life, astonishing Nelson with her stoicism and courage in the face of difficulties. He perhaps could not have chosen a better wife to keep his name alive while he disappeared from view on an Atlantic Ocean prison island.

In 1959 Winnie was charged with and acquitted of taking part in marches. The ANC was banned in 1960 and Nelson went underground, becoming known as the Black Pimpernel. He received military training in Algeria and visited Europe. He was arrested and sentenced to three years in prison in 1962, and she was given the first of her many banning orders, restricting her to Johannesburg and her home from dusk to dawn. In 1963 he was charged and sentenced to life imprisonment with the other Rivonia Trialists (*see* page 32). With most of the ANC leadership in jail or exile, and channels like the International Defence and Aid Fund (IDAF) that operated from London still being set up, Winnie battled financially. Amin Cajee employed her in his cobbler's shop, but security police surveillance and harassment was so intense, that she offered to leave when she saw his business suffering. This pattern was repeated over and over until a photographic supply company, Frank & Hirsch, decided to ignore the harassment and employ her. They continued paying her even when she was banished to Brandfort in the Free State in 1977.

Her children often stayed with the family of Ama, Roy and Indres Naidoo or Helen Joseph, who scraped together their meagre resources to assist Winnie and the girls. Later IDAF helped send the girls to a fine boarding school in Swaziland, far enough away from the attentions of South African security police but close enough to visit Winnie occasionally.

Nelson, in prison, saw Zindzi in 1975 and had a contact visit with Zenani after her marriage at the end of the 1970s, but it was 21 years before he and Winnie were allowed a contact visit. In the early years he was allowed only two visits a year, of half an hour each. They would speak into microphones and gaze at each other through narrow windows with thick glass. The visits were monitored and if either said anything the authorities found unacceptable a screen would crash down, and future visits and letters (five a year) would be jeopardized.

Winnie was a favoured quarry of the security police. On 12 May 1969, she was detained with 22 people under the 1967 Terrorism Act. When the police arrived, she was alone with Zenani and Zindzi, both under the age of 10. The police were rough with the girls and refused to allow Winnie to call anyone to look after them. 'For 17 months I did not know what had happened to my girls. For me that was

OPPOSITE: Nelson Mandela and Winnie Nomzamo Madikizela on their wedding day, on 14 June 1958.

BELOW: Nelson and Winnie Mandela – their embraces were to be short-lived.

ABOVE: *Winnie Mandela with her young daughters Zenani and Zindzi.*

OPPOSITE: *Winnie and Zindzi after Winnie was banished to Brandfort.*

the worst torture,' she recalled. In detention, she and many other women were kept naked, not given sanitary towels and not allowed to clean, so that menstrual blood caked on their legs.

In 1991 Winnie said, 'I went through what everyone else did ... torture and detention.' The evidence of 12,500 applicants before the Truth and Reconciliation Commission (TRC) and the testimony of 7,500 victims who told of torture, disappearances, death and state harassment showed how extensive and cruel that treatment was. And that no two people cope with events in the same way. Post-traumatic stress syndrome, common to people tortured or incarcerated, can be repressed for long periods but can cause violent behaviour when triggered by stress. Primo Levi, an Italian Jew interned at Auschwitz, wrote: 'Those who are tortured remain tortured ... gratuitous violence ... refuses to be forgotten.' It not only refuses to be forgotten, it sometimes fills the victims with a desire for revenge.

On 16 June 1976, Soweto school pupils, protesting against Afrikaans as a medium of instruction, were shot at by police. Over the next months thousands were wounded and more than 500 killed (*see also* page 37). Winnie and other parents came strongly to the fore under the Black Consciousness Black Parents Convention, which again saw her and many others detained. Mandela applauded Winnie's decision to work with black organizations which had political ideologies different from the ANC. He indicated this in a speech smuggled to the ANC which took two years to reach Lusaka: 'The first condition for victory is black unity. Every effort to divide the blacks, to woo and pit one black group against another, must be vigorously repulsed. Our people – African, coloured, Indian and democratic whites – must be united into a single massive and solid wall of resistance ... .' With this call, Mandela planted a seed in the ANC that led to the formation in 1983 of the most successful legal resistance movement ever in South Africa, the United Democratic Front (UDF).

Intensifying his call for united action, Mandela wrote: 'The dead live on as martyrs in our hearts and minds, a reproach to our disunity and the host of shortcomings that accompany divisions among the oppressed, a spur to our efforts to close ranks, and a reminder that the freedom of our people is yet to be won.' To Winnie, he wrote passionate, sometimes lovesick, letters, commending her courage and initiative, yearning for her visits, and asking after their children. He would appeal to friends such as Helen Joseph to take care of Winnie. In return they would send him news of his family. They also sent messages to him through other prisoners or communicated through coded messages via visitors.

In May 1977, Winnie was banished to Brandfort, a dusty Free State village. Her house was tiny, but had enough space for her later to build, with donations from American admirers, a small clinic where she treated local people. Each day at 11 a.m. she waited at the post office at a public telephone for calls from around the world. Initially she was desperately lonely. Zindzi stayed with her for a while but she had her own life to lead. Brandfort residents were divided between those who helped her and those who feared that kindness would lead to a visit from the security police. Her visitors were routinely arrested and some were jailed.

I have often wondered whether any kind of commitment can ever be sufficient excuse for abandoning a young and inexperienced woman in a pitiless desert.

NELSON MANDELA

Zindzi and Winnie during Winnie's banishment to Brandfort, 1977.

ABOVE: In 1984 Winnie defied the banning orders which restricted her to Brandfort and returned to Johannesburg.

OPPOSITE: Nelson Mandela turned his Island cell into a home graced with a photograph of his wife and tomatoes from the garden which fellow prisoner Elias Motsoaledi lovingly cultivated from pips and smuggled seeds.

Nelson urged her to remain courageous in his letters: 'Had it not been for your visits, wonderful letters and your love, I would have fallen apart many years ago.' Foreign dignitaries and diplomats began visiting her, the most important of whom was Senator Edward Kennedy of the United States of America in 1984, with a huge media contingent in tow. No-one in the ANC was as powerful as Winnie in drawing the press, or as skilful in playing them.

In the end, however, the media turned on her. By the early 1980s reports were coming out of Brandfort of brawls, affairs, a community divided between anger and loyalty toward her. At first those on the left dismissed these as state disinformation, but investigations by ANC sympathizers showed many complaints and rumours to have substance. A conspiracy of silence began, with left-leaning journalists her most important protectors. When Winnie defied her banning order and returned to Johannesburg in 1984, it was a dream come true for the security police. In the flesh she was arrogant and unpredictable. Her romantic image began crumbling. The government hastened this by lifting her banning and banishment orders so that she could be freely quoted, and Winnie slowly became her own worst enemy.

The townships were becoming war zones. In 1984 ANC supporters in Duduza, accusing Maki Skosana of being a police informer (the TRC revealed they were wrong), beat her and pushed her to the ground. Someone placed a tyre around her neck; others poured petrol over her. A match was lit. While her screams rent the air and bricks and rocks were thrown at her, she burned to death. That night her execution was shown on South African television.

Throughout 1984 and 1985 dozens of government collaborators and police informers were executed by the 'necklace'. Some hardened media people could not bear to go into the townships, because of the gruesome sights they saw. On 8 January 1986, ANC president Oliver Tambo called for an end to necklacing. It stopped, but a month later, at a funeral for victims of police shootings in Mamelodi, Winnie lifted her fist before the crowd and said, 'With our matches and necklaces we will liberate South Africa.' Black South Africans argued over which call was more valid. The ANC in Lusaka was livid and told her to keep her mouth shut (a message which they would repeat more than once) and to stop contradicting ANC policy. That year Mandela summoned Winnie to Cape Town where he berated her.

I had hoped to build you a refuge, no matter how small, so that we would have a place for rest and sustenance before the arrival of the sad, dry days.

NELSON MANDELA IN A LETTER WRITTEN TO WINNIE FROM ROBBEN ISLAND

ABOVE: Winnie Madikizela-Mandela during her 1997 Truth and Reconciliation Commission hearings.

OPPOSITE TOP: Stompie Seipei, murdered by the Mandela United Football Club with the complicity of Winnie Madikizela-Mandela.

OPPOSITE BOTTOM: The late Lolo Sono and Sibusiso Shabalala (second from right and right). The TRC found that Madikizela-Mandela was involved in Sono's abduction and knew that both men were held on her premises.

The Mandela United Football Club (MUFC), which appears to have played no more than two matches in the five years or so of its existence, had been formed. Winnie and its members were often seen travelling around Soweto or to political events in minibuses, the boys wearing tracksuits in ANC colours and Winnie camouflage military-style outfits.

In 1986, over 30,000 South Africans were detained by the security forces. More than 40 percent were children, some as young as eight. Three, aged 11, 13 and 15, died in police custody within nine days of their detention. Electric shocks were applied to the genitals, wrists, nipples and earlobes of children as young as ten.

For nine months, from 1986 to 1987, I computerized and kept the records of the Detainees' Parents' Support Committee (DPSC). When I began, 10-year-old Stompie Seipei had been detained for some time. Occasionally I deleted names from the list, but Stompie's remained until media exposure to the plight of children forced his release. In 1989, the month after his body was found, after it was known that Winnie had removed him from the manse of a Methodist minister, I wrote in the *Los Angeles Times*, 'Stompie Seipei was a strong, brave little boy, far older than his years who saw one too many bodies shot in the street outside his home. He learned too many truths, too early.

'So many children have died in the South African conflict. It will take us decades to fill the hole this has left in our society. Among the most tragic is the death of Stompie Seipei, badly beaten, his throat slit. ...Winnie Mandela has been revered and feted less for herself than for what she symbolizes, Nelson Mandela, a man beloved by his people. He holds extraordinary power over the hearts of South Africans against apartheid. He is the symbolic key to the liberation of all South Africans. His incarceration symbolizes the imprisonment of all South Africans behind the high walls of apartheid. His release would signify the release of black South Africans. It would, I believe, set in motion an unstoppable wave heralding the final days of apartheid. For most of the more than three decades that Winnie Mandela has had to be a papier mâché mask for someone else, she has done a worthy job. Her rebellion is probably not only intense hatred of the regime that has persecuted her for marrying the man racists most fear, but a heartfelt cry from a woman who has never been allowed to be herself. Yet none of this excuses her role in the abduction of four youths and the ultimate murder of 14-year-old Stompie Mokhetsi Seipei.'

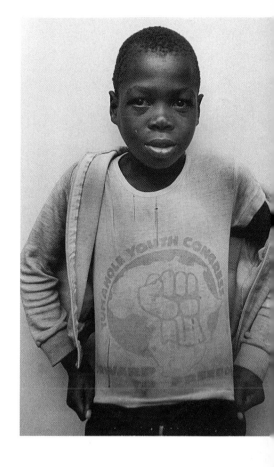

When Stompie's body was found, it showed signs of a savage beating; his throat was slit and punctured. Winnie and a few of her associates were charged with his death. The Appeal Court reduced the sentence to a R15,000 (about US $2,500) fine.

At Winnie's behest the TRC conducted an open hearing into the allegations in December 1997, a hearing that dragged on for two emotionally draining weeks. A TRC poster on the wall read: 'Some of the crimes of our past: Murder, Abduction, Torture'. All were alleged in the two weeks of hearings into the activities of the MUFC and Winnie Madikizela-Mandela (a name she took after her divorce from Mandela; *see* below). Evidence was heard about 19 deaths and 16 assaults, but it was clear there were more.

Mandela had adopted an impassive appearance while sitting beside Winnie at her trial in 1991. He kept silent as newspapers recorded stores suing her for unpaid-for spending sprees and allegations of her misusing ANC funds. Nevertheless, during that time Mandela was being wounded and was forced to suffer the embarrassed shame of his colleagues.

Mandela's wounds began bleeding, but he tried to ignore them, believing 'love does not keep a record of wrongs'. It took him time to remember 'love is happy with the truth' and love gives up when patience and trust, through prolonged abuse, fail. He told the divorce hearing in 1996, 'The bedroom is where a man and a woman discuss the most intimate things. There were so many things I wanted to discuss with her, but she ... never responded to my invitations. I was the loneliest man during the period that I stayed with her.'

On 13 April 1992 he announced his separation from Winnie. Visibly sad, he told the media, 'Ladies and gentlemen, I hope you will appreciate the pain I have gone through.' The ailing Oliver Tambo and Walter Sisulu were at his side as he falteringly read a statement in the boardroom at ANC headquarters at Shell House, Johannesburg: 'Her tenacity reinforced my personal respect, love and growing affection. My love for her remains undiminished.' But 'tensions' had arisen between them.

They had spent less than four years of their 34-year marriage together. Archbishop Desmond Tutu has known both of them since the 1950s, his Johannesburg home a short walk from the Mandelas' in Orlando West. His face is sad and tired when he recalls, 'Nelson doted on Winnie. She has been a very powerful person and I want us to pay a tribute to her for what she stood for in those dark days when they wanted to destroy her. I would not easily condemn her. None of us can predict the pressure we can withstand. I'm still very fond of her.

'I got into trouble with the press when I said he is looking for someone to bring him his slippers. I meant he is looking for a relationship where he has someone who cares for him. He found her in Graça. She is a fabulous woman. She is all the things you want in a woman in many ways and is no doormat. I went to see him on one occasion after he had an operation on his knee. It was 11 a.m. and he was beaming because he was talking to her on the phone. Teenagers have nothing on them. She will remove a fleck off his shirt. I told him, "She really is very caring." He was delighted; he said, "Ah, you have noticed." Let me tell you, males are the most insecure people God created. And Mandela has found just the right sort of woman. When some people nominated her for the post of Secretary-General of the United Nations it was not a sop to her. She is one of the most highly motivated and intelligent women on this continent. Graça was Minister of Education in Mozambique and yet she so typifies her name. She is gracious. She is so solicitous of Leah [Archbishop Tutu's wife] and I when we visit. Their relationship is a gift from heaven for both.'

On 18 July 1998, Nelson Mandela's eightieth birthday and after a week of denying media speculation, Mandela married his official companion and Mozambique's former first lady, Graça Sabine Machel, who is 28 years his junior. They had not even let their children into the secret and after lunch had a brief and moving ceremony.

The first time Nelson Mandela reached out to Graça was in a message smuggled from prison after the death of her husband, Mozambican President Samora Machel, in a plane crash over South African soil in 1986. This crash was probably caused by South African agents working with Mozambican dissidents to interfere with the aircraft's navigational equipment. Mandela was deeply moved by the death of Machel, who had bravely supported the South African liberation struggle. The message, signed by Nelson and Winnie Mandela, was broadcast on Maputo radio on 28 October 1986: 'We have never in our lives submitted a request to leave South Africa, but we believe that today we should be physically present near you. We are both detained in different jails. We have been prevented from being with you today to share your grief, to cry with you, to alleviate your sorrow, to tenderly embrace you. Our grief for the loss of Comrade Samora is so deep that it breaks our hearts. Throughout the night we shall join you in the vigil.

He said to me that he was never so unhappy as in the period after he was released until he decided to leave Soweto.

ARCHBISHOP DESMOND TUTU, 1998

OPPOSITE: Archbishop Tutu during Winnie Madikizela-Mandela's 1997 Truth and Reconciliation hearings.

BELOW: Oliver Tambo (wearing sunglasses) with Samora Machel, the Mozambican president whose aircraft crashed over South African soil in suspicious circumstances in 1986.

Throughout the day we shall cry with you for the loss of that powerful soldier, courageous son and noble statesman. We must believe that his death will give new strength to your and our determination to someday be free. For you it will be through victory over the immoral and lackey bandits. For us it will be a victory over oppression. Our struggle has always been linked and together we shall emerge victorious.'

The relationship between Nelson Mandela and Graça Machel developed slowly after they met in 1990, when he went to Mozambique shortly after his release from prison. Part of the reason for his visit was to meet Graça at the behest of the ailing ANC leader Oliver Tambo. Samora Machel had asked Oliver Tambo to look after his wife and children if anything should happen to him. Tambo, weakened by a stroke, asked Mandela to take over the protective role.

ABOVE AND OPPOSITE: In Graça Machel, Nelson Mandela found a healer of wounds, and South Africa gained a first lady who led by example.

I went to see him on one occasion when he had a knee operation ... he was speaking on the phone to Graça in New York. He was beaming because he was talking to her on the phone. Teenagers have nothing on them.

ARCHBISHOP DESMOND TUTU, 1998

Graça says frankly, 'It was not exactly love at first sight.' But over time they discovered that they had much in common. He invited her daughter Josina to live in his home in Johannesburg while she studied at the University of the Witwatersrand. Partly through that connection, their relationship developed. Graça describes Machel and Mandela both as distinctive men, but with many similar qualities. 'Sometimes when I listen to Nelson I even believe that it is Samora that speaks.' Graça muses that their shared experiences of pain has given them an understanding: 'We enjoy this relationship with such fulfilment and such plenitude. It's so sweet and so complete and so normal. We know what the value is. We don't take it for granted. We know what it is to be without. We say to each other: "At last we are very lucky people because we could have ended up without being able to share this experience." '

The friendship of this strong, warm woman helped Mandela through the pain of his broken relationship with Winnie. Graça does not enter a room with the same drama and charm as Winnie, and is more low-key.

The couple have a strong commitment to the rights of children. The children's fund started by Nelson Mandela is the largest welfare organization in South Africa. Graça is internationally known and respected for her United Nations-sponsored studies of the impact of war on children. During Mozambique's long war for independence from the Portuguese, the Front for the Liberation of Mozambique (Frelimo) set up schools in liberated territories

and in their training camps in Tanzania. Graça participated in the armed struggle, and in 1974 was appointed Deputy Director of the Frelimo Secondary School at Bagamoyo, Tanzania. When Frelimo formed an independent government in 1975, Graça, aged 29, became a member of Frelimo's Central Committee and the Minister of Education and Culture. The only woman in the cabinet, she retained her post for 14 years. In September 1975, she married Samora Machel, the first President of Mozambique, accepting as her own the four children from his marriage to his late wife. Samora and Graça had two children together.

Her work with and for children received high recognition when, in 1994, United Nations Secretary-General Boutros Boutros-Ghali appointed her to chair a study on the Impact of Armed Conflict on Children, the first study of its kind.

Graça, who has ardently campaigned for women's rights, said during the keynote address at a Civitas conference in Pretoria in 1997: 'Gender-based violence is ... one of the world's most pressing issues and this same violence, directed against children during armed conflict, is its most horrible manifestation. ... Exposing children to atrocities, destroying homes, interferes with the development of a child's identity while often simultaneously robbing them of necessary parental guidance. We have to accept the responsibility that we have brought up a generation of youngsters who believe that to achieve something you have to use violence. Our children are becoming accustomed to, and are actively integrated into, this culture of violence. That's why we see gangs which are organized, banditry rising and hijacking and armed robberies mounting. In my country, it's much easier to get a gun than to buy a book for a child. The demilitarization of society is a crucial factor in countering the culture of violence. Our armed forces have stopped making war but our societies remain heavily armed. Equally important is the need to disarm the population and demilitarize their minds to accept a peaceful way of relationships. We need to teach our children and youth that violence should never, but never again, be used to solve differences. Peaceful means, through dialogue and negotiations, is an issue that learning institutions from primary schools to universities need to address.'

'Meanwhile,' Corinthians 13 concludes, 'these three remain: faith, hope and love: and the greatest of these is love.' Nelson Mandela and Graça Machel, who have retained faith and hope in a world that seemed determined to rob them of those qualities, have found the greatest gift of all in each other.

LEFT: Nelson Mandela and Graça Machel at celebrations the day after their wedding on 18 July 1998.

PAGES 58 AND 59: Nelson Mandela said that he missed children more than anything else while he was in prison, particularly on Robben Island, and children respond readily to his 'Madiba magic'.

The influence of prison

Did I make the right decision in leaving my family and letting my children grow up without security? Wounds that cannot be seen are more painful than those that can be seen.

<small>NELSON MANDELA</small>

PAGES 60 AND 61: *Nelson Mandela at the Robben Island lime quarry during a visit by the Rivonia Trialists.*

BELOW: A mass funeral for the victims of the 1960 Sharpeville massacre. Demonstrating against pass laws, which required African people to carry pass books at all times, a peaceful crowd of several thousand people surrounded the police station at Sharpeville near Johannesburg. Panicking, the police force of 75 opened fire on them, killing 69 and wounding hundreds more. Most were shot in the back as they fled.

OPPOSITE: Nelson Mandela burning his pass book in protest at the Sharpeville shootings.

Nelson Mandela's cell on Robben Island, which was the colour of a jade sea under a stormy sky, is little more than three paces wide and five long. Its high narrow window looks onto an exercise yard next to grape arbours, peach trees and a few flowers grown from pips and smuggled seeds. Visiting the prison in 1998, Mandela gazed into the cell where he spent two decades and mused, 'It seems so small now, but so big then'. And it was. He brought the universe into his cell: books, reflections on political debates, analyses of news broadcasts from smuggled radios, snippets of news from contraband newspapers and journals.

Payment for smuggling was often diamonds – obtained by Umkhonto we Sizwe (MK) cadres from Angolan diggings or rivers – which were either given to warders or sold. 'One warder now has a beautiful house on Signal Hill in Cape Town,' reflected Mbeko Zwelakhe, a former MK soldier involved in smuggling operations, who today runs a security company.

In prison Mandela learnt the lessons of survival which he taught to others: 'Prison is designed to break one's spirit and destroy one's resolve. To do this, the authorities attempt to exploit every weakness, demolish every initiative, negate all signs of individuality. Our survival depended on understanding what the authorities were attempting to do to us, and sharing that understanding with each other. It would be very hard, if not impossible, for one man alone to resist. But the authorities' greatest mistake was to keep us together, for together our determination was reinforced. We supported each other and gained strength from each other. Whatever we knew, whatever we learned, we shared and by sharing we multiplied whatever courage we had individually.'

Tokyo Sexwale, who later became the first premier of Gauteng and a successful businessperson, was jailed in the same section as Mandela. He says, 'There are four things you have to learn as a prisoner. First, there are the walls. You ... can see the walls and forever be a prisoner, or you can break through ... and have the whole world before you in your mind. The second challenge is the warders. Some were very harsh. Torture was not uncommon. But you had to work with them every day, and it might take years, but you had to turn them and change them, because they would become important for smuggling. ... The third challenge is your friends and comrades. You live at very close quarters with people you may have worked with outside, but living so close together under such difficult conditions brings out the best and worst in people. Some people you were very close to outside are impossible to live with in prison. And the fourth, and greatest, challenge is yourself. The enemy within. You have to work with and change yourself.'

Mandela said the enemy within makes you ask, 'Did I make the right decision in leaving my family and letting my children grow up without security? Although I agonized over my family, I was still convinced that even if I had known how serious the consequence of my acts I would have done the same.' That realization did not ease a

sense of guilt and sadness. His mother died while he was in prison and he was refused permission to bury her. 'The next shattering experience was the death of my oldest son in a car accident. He was not just a son but a friend. The warders used psychological persecution – whenever something happened to my family, I would come from the quarry and find a newspaper cutting on my desk.'

Before prison Mandela was a gifted leader who tended to arrogance. Prison hardship taught him patience; the denial of rights – wisdom; the empathy of others less privileged than himself – compassion. Prison made him one of the greatest leaders of history.

In April 1969, Mandela embarked upon the first of many initiatives over almost 15 years to begin talks with government. He wrote asking for his release and that of his comrades, or their recognition as political prisoners. He pointed to the lenient treatment meted out to Boer rebels and Nazi-sympathizing Afrikaners in World War II. Government ignored his missive.

Maintaining a rigorous schedule of meetings, talks and discussion seminars, he refused to be imprisoned by his walls, and he refused to be cowed. Accepting India's Jawaharlal Nehru Award in 1980, he wrote a letter that was smuggled to the Indian government from his cell on the Island. Quoting Nehru, he said: 'Walls and dangerous companions ... make you a prisoner and a slave ... [but] the most terrible of walls are the walls ... in the mind, which prevent you from discarding an evil tradition simply because it is old, and from accepting a new thought because it is novel.' The letter gave insights into how prison formed his thinking: 'The politically inclined youth of my generation were drawn together by feelings of an intense, but narrow form of nationalism. ... Time was to teach us as Panditji says, that "nationalism is good in its place, but is an unreliable friend and an unsafe historian. It binds us to many happenings and sometimes distorts the truth." '

This underscored his Presidency: he would bend to catch the whispers of a child, place a caring hand on the shoulder of an old woman, even travel thousands of miles to see Betsie Verwoerd, widow of the architect of apartheid, Hendrik Verwoerd. When he spoke to her, he bent close to her lips, lest he miss a word. The way she glowed in his presence was testimony that his journey was worth it. With one visit he felled the might of right-wing saboteurs.

Patrick 'Terror' Lekota, African National Congress chairperson and head of the National Council of Provinces, who was also incarcerated on the Island, said, 'Prison compels a breadth of your vision and understanding. If you wanted something you had to get on your knees and plead with someone. This compels you to a sense of God, of you not being in total control of everything. There is a recognition that sometimes you have to depend on some other force, real or imagined. Anyone who goes to jail and is subject to those conditions learns humility. Prison tempered a lot of the animal instincts in us. Prison and age. You mix with people you never would have if you had not gone to jail. You share the same ablution facilities, eat the same porridge from the same plate, share the same blankets, you talk to people and discover that although they are not from the same social background they have much to offer.'

Mandela learnt in prison that the humblest people can sometimes have the greatest insights. Mac Maharaj, former Minister of Transport, says, 'His genius was that he gave leadership to a disparate body of prisoners to act in concert to improve prison conditions. But he never made prison conditions the sole reason for any interaction as there was always a greater political purpose. Madiba also conducted himself in such a way that the authorities could never have the excuse to close the door on him.'

Mandela and his elder son, Madiba Thembekile (Thembi), who died in a road accident at the age of 25 while Mandela was on the Island.

This was how he achieved a negotiated settlement for South Africa. It is clear that the National Party (Nats) had believed that they could corral the African National Congress by unbanning it and allowing free political activity. At the same time government promoted state death squads, gun-running and the provocation of massive violence in black areas to force, so they hoped, black people to long for the firm leadership of the Nats and white rule – the 'quiet of apartheid'. By the same token the chaos was supposed to affirm to white people and to the international community that black South Africans were not only incapable of ruling South Africa but, left to their own devices, would cause the genocidal mayhem that has been seen in other parts of Africa.

GOD'S SWORD

Nelson Mandela, with his willingness to talk to his enemies, to give them allowances that even their own would not give, subverted the plans of a white minority government which believed war and conflict would give it the upper hand. One of the men who was central to the decision to release Mandela, and in talks leading to the unbanning of the African National Congress, was Lukas Daniël (Niel) Barnard, a former professor of the Political Science Department at the University of the Orange Free State. His views were a perfect fit for the new government of Pieter Willem Botha who, in 1979, succeeded Balthazar John Vorster as President. Vorster's government had not seen the 16 June 1976 Soweto student uprising coming, despite Zulu leader Mangosuthu Buthelezi's eerie prophecy precisely three months before the uprising that 'South Africa is approaching its hour of crisis'.

PW Botha, while promising reform, handpicked as head of the National Intelligence Service (NIS) 31-year-old Barnard, making him the youngest spymaster in South Africa's history.

Barnard regaled journalists with his writings, which were peppered with biblical allusions to 'the sword of God' – in Afrikaans, military power is often referred to as *swaardmag* (sword power). He wrote: 'In world politics fragmented by sin, the sword must always be applied justifiably for the punishment of evil. The attitude that the Christian state must never take up the sword and suffer for justice, is dangerous cowardice.'

South Africa began launching raids against its neighbours (Lesotho, Botswana, Swaziland, Mozambique, Zambia and Zimbabwe), purportedly against ANC guerrillas, but killing anyone in their way. In one raid at Matola in 1981, 13 ANC members were executed by South African soldiers in swastika-emblazoned helmets. The ears of the dead soldiers were cut off and given to their commanders. Under Barnard and those of his ilk in the military security establishment, death squads emerged and South Africa's chemical and biological warfare programme was honed. These squads developed poisoned t-shirts, anthrax-tipped cigarettes, teargas made out of marijuana, ecstasy and LSD. Shortly before Mandela's release in 1990 they plotted to murder him with an untraceable compound that would destroy brain cells. It was with these people that Mandela would need to negotiate.

In May 1983, the heart of Afrikanerdom and the soul of whites were shaken by a car bomb explosion outside airforce headquarters in Pretoria at rush hour, a blast which killed 19 and injured 215. Police cordoned off the area as black smoke billowed above the city and radio stations interrupted all programmes. At the HF Verwoerd

The renowned finger of President PW Botha, whose cabinet forced his resignation in 1989.

Hospital, dazed relatives wandered the hallways clutching each other and sobbing as wave after wave of ambulances screeched to a halt at the casualty entrance. This was an alarm which South Africa heeded – though it made many whites more belligerent. The ANC, which had earlier launched a rocket attack against Voortrekkerhoogte military base and Sasol oil refineries, said it would remain focused on military targets but in some instances civilian casualties would result. It was a clarion call to increased conflict and resistance which initially grew under the yellow, red and black banners of the United Democratic Front (UDF). Launched that August, the UDF embraced 700 anti-apartheid organizations, many mainly white.

PW Botha's reform initiatives, balanced with increasing repression, had yet to impress the international community, and the release of Mandela was becoming essential to real progress. In March 1984, over 4,000 foreign celebrities signed a petition calling for his release. Government ignored it and went on trying to root out ANC bases from the Frontline States (Mozambique, Angola, Zimbabwe, Zambia, Tanzania, Swaziland and Lesotho).

Robben Island, where Nelson Mandela was incarcerated for more than two decades until 1982, with Table Mountain in the background. The prison is located in the middle of the left side of the Island.

WE SALUTE THE HUNGER STRIKERS!
FREE ALL SOUTH AFRICAN
FREE ALL SOUTH AFRICAN DETAINEES
FREE ALL SOUTH AFRICAN DETAINEES

In September 1983, complaints about Nelson Mandela's incarceration at Pollsmoor came before a United Nations Human Rights Commission (UNHRC). Testimony was given that Mandela shared a damp cell with five other prisoners, which made it difficult for him to study. Two months later, apparently in response to the UNHRC hearing, but more likely to promote the secret talks process, Mandela was separated from the other prisoners. Mandela recalls, 'I thought I should approach the government and ask for a meeting between government and the ANC – because we are products of a collective leadership. I agonized over the fact that I would approach the government without discussing the matter with my colleagues, comrades Sisulu, Kathrada, Mlangeni ... but I felt that if I did they would reject my move, because of our hatred of National Party politicians. However, I thought the time was right for negotiations. My comrades did not have the advantages I had of brushing shoulders with the VIP's that came to prison, judges, the Minister of Justice, the Commissioner of Prisons.

'I decided to confront my colleagues with a fait accompli, so I approached the government and had discussions over some time with Mr Kobie Coetsee, who said discussions must be secret. I said confidential yes, but secret no. I reached a stage where I wanted to see my four comrades who were with me in Pollsmoor. The authorities refused and said see them one by one, so I called ... comrade Walter Sisulu. I calculated that if I convinced him he would help me convince the rest. He ... said Madiba, I have nothing against negotiations, but I would prefer that they start first, not us. I said Comrade Tshepo [which means hope] if you are not against negotiations, it doesn't matter who starts. Raymond Mhlaba said, what were you waiting for all this time, you should have done this long ago. Comrade Kathrada said he disagreed with me. Comrade Mlangeni agreed. Then I smuggled a letter to the leadership outside. A reply came back from Oliver Tambo, there was a note of disapproval, he said what are you discussing with these fellows? I said, I am discussing a meeting with the ANC and government, just one line. I told them later in a memo that I was discussing violence, negotiations, the alliance with the SACP [South African Communist Party], the question of majority rule. The ANC said it was the right thing to do and authorized me. Then I called comrades from Natal, the Transvaal, the Orange Free State and the Cape, members of the ANC, the youth league, the women's league and members of trade unions. I briefed them and no-one said no, I called the prisoners [the remaining Rivonia Trialists] from Robben Island too.

'The government appointed a top level team of negotiators: General Willemse, Kobie Coetsee, Niel Barnard, then head of the National Intelligence Service, constitutional expert Fanie van der Merwe and Mike Louw of NIS. Then I saw PW in mid-1989. It was one of the best meetings I have ever had, he received me very well. I was removed from Pollsmoor to Victor Verster. Those were the best days in prison, because it was a stage between prison and freedom.' General Willemse, who became Commissioner of Prisons in 1983 and who had known Mandela since 1971 while he was commanding officer on the Island, said the meetings took place at Pollsmoor in VIP guest houses, in the VIP dining room, in the club-house, once in General Willemse's home within Pollsmoor precincts. Other meetings occurred at the home of Kobie Coetsee – he and Mandela once even played tennis – and at Victor Verster prison.

But, to the outside world, things were getting worse, not better. On 20 July 1985 a State of Emergency was declared in 36 black urban areas. In the first week 1,000 people were detained. On 15 August the world media cleared their airwaves for a speech which government said would introduce radical reforms. Instead, in his 'Rubicon' speech, Botha delivered

We have set out on a quest for true humanity, and somewhere on the distant horizon we can see the glittering prize. Let us march forth with courage and determination, drawing strength from our common plight and our brotherhood. In time we shall bestow upon South Africa the greatest gift possible – a more human face.

STEVEN BANTU BIKO (BLACK CONSCIOUSNESS LEADER MURDERED BY POLICE WHILE IN DETENTION), SEPTEMBER 1977

OPPOSITE: The late Archbishop Trevor Huddleston leads a prayer vigil in London.

Nelson Mandela and the Rivonia Trialists escaped the noose but many others were not as lucky. By the 1980s South Africa had the highest rate of executions in the world. In just one week before Christmas 1987, 21 people were hanged. Here 'young lions' (from left: Tenki Sekonye, Rapu Malekane, Peter Mokaba and a representative of the South African National Student Congress) protest against executions in July 1987 in front of a banner proclaiming the ANC Youth League's commitment to victory at all costs.

a belligerent, blustering apologia for apartheid. Within days the currency dropped to almost a third of its value. Academics, newspaper editors and businesspeople began meeting with the ANC, despite government threats to seize their passports. Harry Oppenheimer, South Africa's wealthiest man, publicly came out in support of Mandela's release. On 21 November 1985, the ANC stepped up the pressure by presenting their conditions for negotiations, in the Harare Declaration. This document demanded the release of Mandela and other political prisoners, the lifting of the State of Emergency, the withdrawal of troops from townships, the unbanning of the ANC and the creation of conditions for free political activity.

Publicly the government said it would talk with the ANC only if it renounced violence; the ANC responded by saying government also had to renounce violence. Mac Maharaj muses: 'We brought democracy to our country, but not within the textbook theory of

A message of solidarity etched into the wet cement of the Island's breakwater wall.

revolution that we had cut our teeth on politically in the 1950s, as the world had fundamentally changed by the mid-1980s. But whatever the changes are, history writes down as its leaders the men and women who have both the ability to detect its shifts and the courage to act on it. This is a measure of the leadership of Nelson Mandela, who decided in the isolation of his prison cell to take the initiative and open dialogue with the hated apartheid regime. ... History will record that Madiba ... read the moment correctly. ... Every lonely step he took to set up the preconditions

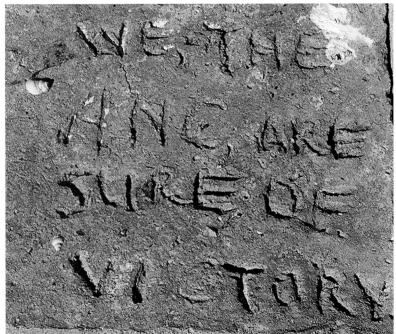

I'm a leader by default, says Tutu

By Jo-Anne Collinge

Two men dominated the gathering of thousands in Soweto yesterday when the Nobel Peace Prize was brought "home" to the people of South Africa.

They were Bishop Desmond Tutu, who stood before the crowd with the prize medal in his hand, and Nelson Mandela, more than a thousand kilometres away in a prison cell in Cape Town.

Bishop Tutu, head of the Anglican Diocese of Johannesburg and patron of the United Democratic Front (UDF), said he and others like him were leaders by default — because the true leaders had been jailed or exiled.

"Many of you young people here have never heard the likes of Nelson Mandela, Walter Sisulu or Oliver Tambo speak," he told the crowd in the massive UDF rally organised in his honour.

"These are the people the system says have been put into cold storage. But when I say to you: 'Who are your leaders?' — there is absolutely no doubt."

Applause and chanting made clear the support the jailed and exiled African National Congress men command.

The bishop said the popular leaders of South Africa were not bloodthirsty, and were honoured elsewhere in the world.

The bishop warned: "There is no hope for peace in this land until they (the present rulers) talk to our leaders."

Inkatha against disinvestment

Chief Gatsha Buthelezi's Inkatha Movement yesterday joined the call for the unconditional release of African National Congress (ANC) leader, Nelson Mandela, at its East Rand regional meeting at the Kwesine Hostel hall in Katlehong, Germiston.

The region also supported the call to overseas firms not to disinvest. Members said they believed disinvestment would only bring hardships for blacks.

The region's Youth Brigade planned to embark on a campaign to keep the environment clean, as part of the International Youth Year project.

Moments of drama during the United Democratic Front's mass rally in Soweto at the weekend. Left: Nobel laureate Bishop Desmond Tutu holds the Peace Prize medal up to the crowd, saying: "Take it, it's yours." Right: Zinzi Mandela, daughter of Nelson, brings her father's message from jail: "I cannot sell my birthright, nor the birthright of the people to be free." Pictures by Juda Ngwenya

First unban the ANC — Mandela

This is the full text of Nelson Mandela's response to the conditional offer of freedom made in Parliament by the State President, Mr P W Botha. It was read by his daughter Zinzi.

"On Friday my mother and our attorney saw my father at Pollsmoor Prison to obtain his answer to Botha's offer of conditional release.

"The prison authorities attempted to stop this statement being made but he would have none of this and made it clear that he would make the statement to you, the people.

"Strangers like Bethell from England and Professor Dash from the United States have in recent weeks been authorised by Pretoria to see my father without restriction yet Pretoria cannot allow you, the people, to hear what he has to say directly. He should be here himself to tell you what he thinks of this statement by Botha. He is not allowed to do so. My mother who also heard his words is also not allowed to speak to you today.

"My father and his comrades at Pollsmoor Prison send their greetings to you, the freedom-loving people of this, our tragic land in the full confidence that you will carry on the struggle for freedom.

"He, with his comrades at Pollsmoor Prison, sends his very warmest greetings to Bishop Tutu. Bishop Tutu has made it clear to the world that the Nobel Peace Prize belongs to you, who are the people. We salute him.

"My father and his comrades at Pollsmoor Prison are grateful to the United Democratic Front, who without hesitation made this venue available to them so that they could speak to you today.

"My father and his comrades wish to make this statement to you, the people, first. They are clear that they are accountable to you and to you alone. And that you should hear their views directly and not through others.

"My father speaks not only for himself and for his comrades at Pollsmoor Prison but he hopes he also speaks for all those in jail for their opposition to apartheid, for all those who are banished, for all those who are in exile, for all those who suffer under apartheid, for all those who are opponents of apartheid and for all those who are oppressed and exploited. Throughout our struggle there have been

Rejection hits UK headlines

The Star Bureau

LONDON — Nelson Mandela's rejection of President Botha's offer of conditional release is prominently reported in most Fleet Street newspapers today.

The Daily Telegraph, makes it front-page news under the headline, "Mandela rejects lure of freedom". The Times publishes a front-page photograph of Bishop Desmond Tutu with Mandela's daughter, Zindzi, and The Guardian places the same photograph on an inside page.

The statement was also featured on radio and television.

Several correspondents note that Mandela appeared to leave open the possibility of negotiations with the Government.

puppets who have claimed to speak for you. They have made this claim, both here and abroad. They are of no consequence. My father and his colleagues will not be like them.

"My father says: 'I am a member of the African National Congress. I have always been a member of the African National Congress and I will remain a member of the African National Congress until the day I die. Oliver Tambo is much more than a brother to me. He is my greatest friend and comrade for nearly 50 years. If there is any one amongst you who cherishes my freedom, Oliver Tambo cherishes it more and I know that he would give his life to see me free. There is no difference between his views and mine.'

"My father says: 'I am surprised at the conditions that the Government wants to impose on me. I am not a violent man. My colleagues and I wrote in 1952 to Malan asking for a round-table conference to find a solution to the problems of our country but that was ignored.

'When Strijdom was in power, we made the same offer. Again it was ignored. When Verwoerd was in power we asked for a national convention for all the people in South Africa to decide on their future. This, too, was in vain.

'It was only then when all other forms of resistance were no longer open to us that we turned to armed struggle.

'Let Botha show that he is different to Malan, Strijdom and Verwoerd.

'Let him renounce violence.

'Let him say that he will dismantle apartheid.

'Let him unban the people's organisation, the African National Congress.

'Let him free all who have been imprisoned, banished or exiled for their opposition to apartheid.

'Let him guarantee free political activity so that the people may decide who will govern them.

'I cherish my own freedom dearly but I care even more for your freedom. Too many have died since I went to prison. Too many have suffered for the love of freedom. I owe it to their widows, to their orphans, to their mothers and to their fathers who have grieved and wept for them. Not only I have suffered during these long, lonely, wasted years.

'I am not less life-loving than you are. But I cannot sell my birthright, nor am I prepared to sell the birthright of the people to be free. I am in prison as the representative of the people and of your organisation, the African National Congress, which was banned. What freedom am I being offered while the organisation of the people remains banned? What freedom am I being offered when I may be arrested on a pass offence? What freedom am I being offered to live my life as a family with my dear wife who remains in banishment in Brandfort? What freedom am I being offered when I must ask for permission to live in an urban area? What freedom am I being offered when I need a stamp in my pass to seek work? What freedom am I being offered when my very South African citizenship is not respected?

'Only free men can negotiate. Prisoners cannot enter into contracts. Herman Toivo Ja Toivo, when freed, never gave any undertaking, nor was he called upon to do so.'

"My father says: 'I cannot and will not give any undertaking at a time when I and you the people are not free. Your freedom and mine cannot be separated. I will return.' " — Sapa.

Nelson Mandela's reply to PW Botha's offer of conditional freedom was delivered by his youngest daughter Zindzi on Sunday 10 February 1985 to a crowd at the Jabulani Stadium in Soweto, Johannesburg.

for talks with the apartheid regime was carefully weighed to ensure he did not in any way undermine or compromise the ANC, and that any possible failure in his bold strategy would be borne by him alone without bringing embarrassment to his organization.'

The 'securocrats' of PW Botha developed 'total onslaught' and 'total strategy' claims for the threats that they perceived to be facing South Africa in the early 1980s, justifying a complex military system that encouraged citizens to spy on each other. The State Security Council (SSC), which had been put in place in 1972 under the presidency of John Vorster, became the real government. The committee was one of 20 cabinet committees until 1979. When Botha, who had been defence chief since 1966, became Prime Minister in 1978, he needed to assert control over the powerful Bureau for State Security (BOSS) under General Hendrik van den Bergh, a confidant of Vorster. Botha's sympathies lay with the military, the intelligence arm of which despised BOSS. Since its 1975 invasion of Angola, the military had been at variance with the cabinet. Botha and the military wanted to take the war to the enemy, and

Botha told the public that revolution was a possibility. He and his generals characterized anti-apartheid activity as a total onslaught which only a total strategy could confront.

Barnard wrote in the press: 'Terror is drama ... directed at the greatest possible number of people that can see and hear; definitely not at the greatest number of people that can be killed. To this end, the TV, radio and press is of great assistance to terrorism in the announcement of terror capabilities on the one hand, and the creation of sympathetic public opinion on the other.'

Mandela's contacts with government intensified in July 1984, when Justice Minister Kobie Coetsee visited him in a Cape Town hospital, Constantiaberg, where he was recovering from an illness. On 31 January 1985 PW Botha announced to the House of Assembly: 'The government is willing to consider Mr Mandela's release in the Republic of South Africa on condition that Mr Mandela gives a commitment that he will not make himself guilty of planning, instigating or committing acts of violence for the furtherance of political objectives, but will conduct himself in such a way that he will not again have to be arrested... . It is therefore not the South African government which now stands in the way of Mr Mandela's freedom. It is he himself. The choice is his. All that is required of him now is that he should unconditionally reject violence as a political instrument. This is, after all, a norm which is respected in all civilized countries of the world.'

Winnie Mandela, Dullah Omar and some of Mandela's grandchildren visit him in prison not long before his release.

The influence of prison

On 8 February that same year Winnie Mandela visited her husband with his lawyer Ismail Ayob in order to obtain a reply to the President's offer. Mandela chose to speak to President Botha through an address to the people from whom he had so long been separated. It was a unique opportunity that reaffirmed the centrality of the ANC to any political solution for South Africa. While Ayob and Winnie sat before him, he began to dictate his speech, but a prison warder stopped him. Mandela said he had the right to reply to the President in whatever way he chose. A senior officer then appeared and told Mandela to desist. Mandela told the prison authorities to telephone the President and continued dictating.

On Sunday, 10 February, his youngest daughter Zindzi read her father's statement on a sweltering summer's day at the Jabulani Stadium in Soweto (*see* picture, page 72). The occasion had been planned by the United Democratic Front to celebrate the Nobel Peace Prize that had been awarded to Anglican Bishop Desmond Tutu in Oslo two months previously. Standing before the hushed crowd, Zindzi, dressed in jeans and a t-shirt, read: 'My father and his comrades ... are clear that they are accountable to you and to you alone. And that you should hear their views directly and not through others. He speaks also for all those in jail for their opposition to apartheid, for all those who are banished, for all those who are in exile, for all those who suffer under apartheid, for all those who are opponents of apartheid and for all those who are oppressed and exploited... . He says, I will remain a member of the African National Congress until the day I die. Oliver Tambo is much more than a brother to me. He is my dearest friend and comrade for nearly fifty years. If there is any one among you who cherishes my freedom, Oliver Tambo cherishes it more ... there is no difference between his views and mine... . Let Botha renounce violence. Let him say that he will dismantle apartheid. Let him unban the people's organization,

Nelson Mandela embraces a former prison warder.

the African National Congress. Let him free all who have been imprisoned, banished or exiled for their opposition to apartheid. Let him guarantee free political activity so that the people may decide who will govern them.

'I cherish my own freedom dearly but I care even more for your freedom.... I cannot sell my birthright, nor am I prepared to sell the birthright of the people to be free. What freedom am I being offered while the organization of the people remains banned? What freedom

Rivonia Trialists (from left) Dennis Goldberg, Andrew Mlangeni, Nelson Mandela, Ahmed Kathrada and Walter Sisulu visit Robben Island on 11 February 1994.

The influence of prison

75

His genius was that he gave leadership to a disparate body of prisoners to act in concert to improve prison conditions. But he never made prison conditions the sole reason for any interaction as there was always a greater political purpose. Madiba also conducted himself in such a way that the authorities could never have the excuse to close the door on him.

MAC MAHARAJ (FORMER MINISTER OF TRANSPORT)

Nelson Mandela, two months before he was elected President in April 1994, stares pensively out of the high window of the Robben Island cell in which he was held for two decades.

Nelson Mandela speaks at the Robben Island Museum before a mural depicting some of the leaders of the resistance struggle – Govan Mbeki, Mandela himself, Steve Biko, Robert Sobukwe and Walter Sisulu.

am I being offered when I may be arrested on a pass offence? What freedom am I being offered to live my life as a family with my dear wife who remains in banishment in Brandfort? What freedom am I being offered when I need a stamp in my pass to seek work? What freedom am I being offered when my very South African citizenship is not respected? Only free men can negotiate. Prisoners cannot enter into contracts... . I will return.' The ululating cheering crowd showed his words had been well chosen.

Government was not impressed.

In May 1988, Botha established a four-man committee to handle talks with the ANC leadership; the members were General Willie Willemse (head of prisons), Niel Barnard, Barnard's assistant Mike Louw and Fanie van der Merwe (a constitutional expert). All four had already been involved for some time in talks with Mandela.

On 18 January 1989, Botha suffered a mild stroke and was attended by his personal physician, Dr Wouter Basson, head of Special Forces and its chemical and biological warfare programme (*see* page 94). On 2 February, Botha resigned as head of the National Party; a National Party Federal Council meeting on 13 March called for

sobukwe   sisulu

his resignation as President. A furious Botha announced elections for 6 September 1989 and then, on 5 July, stunned critics by courteously entertaining Mandela to tea and cake at Tuynhuys, the presidential quarters abutting Parliament. Six weeks later Botha was forced to resign by his cabinet.

One of the contenders in the leadership tussle was the conservative Frederick Willem de Klerk, who belonged to a sect of the Reformed Church which was so conservative that its members were not allowed to dance. His wife Marike had in previous speeches been quoted as referring to coloured people as 'non persons' who were South Africa's 'leftovers'. His rival was the long-time Foreign Minister Pik Botha, who was popular in English circles and among more liberal Afrikaners.

As the first blossoms of spring fell off trees and coated newly green lawns with pink and cream showers, FW de Klerk was elected President. Two months later he scrapped the National Security Management System, which organized civilians into officials of the state security system under the SSC. He also downgraded the SSC, thus making the cabinet the highest policy-making body. The stage was set for the arduous transition to democracy.

The path to power

The regime has its own strategy and part of it will be to ensure that Mandela does not bring on a revolution for them.

Oliver Tambo
Emergency Meeting of the ANC
National Working Committee,
28 October 1988

our LEADERS
Mandela
Kathrada
Mbeki
Mhlaba
nd all POLITICAL PRISONERS

NELSON
MANDELA
The struggle
is my life

Mandela
82

The biggest dilemma facing the National Party government in the 1980s was an unwelcome realization that Nelson Mandela's release would symbolize the release of every black South African from apartheid, creating forces that would hasten the end of white minority rule.

The African National Congress (ANC) was concerned that the government might try to lure ANC cadres into South Africa, and trick ANC supporters in the country into revealing themselves, in order to imprison or kill them. While the ANC believed the struggle could be won only by military means, it lacked the forces, equipment and funds to bring about the downfall of the South African government without economic and social destruction.

The 1985 Kabwe Conference, the ANC's first consultative conference in exile since the 1969 Morogoro conference, said it was time 'for us to sue for the expulsion of apartheid South Africa from the UN, to push for practical measures by the international community based on the rejection of the Pretoria regime as illegitimate'. It was perhaps the most important conference of the decade for the ANC. International sanctions against South Africa followed, and the seal was set on the beginning of the end of apartheid.

On 20 July 1985 a partial State of Emergency was declared that soon encompassed the whole country. This would continue for four years, becoming ever more repressive. Four months after the State of Emergency was declared, and with thousands of black South Africans imprisoned, the ANC presented their conditions for negotiations to the National Party government, the Harare Declaration, which became the blueprint for change. South African Deputy Minister of Information Louis Nel dismissed the declaration, saying the government had no intention of having talks with the ANC.

A month later government said it would talk to the ANC and release Mandela if they renounced violence. This condition was rejected. The ANC continued to prepare to assume power, and by 1988 had released a set of constitutional guidelines. This professional approach to the rigours and responsibilities of governing made the ANC unique among liberation movements, and also contributed to the peaceful negotiated transition that followed.

Plans to release Mandela were discussed by the State Security Council (SSC), whose ideas ranged from the bizarre to the sinister. The government leaked news that it might release him in return for the freedom of Soviet dissidents Anatoly Shcharansky and Andrei Sakharov, hoping to win American and Soviet approval. It was ignored. National State Security Council ideas included liberating Mandela outside South Africa, into Transkei or a villa on Robben Island, or freedom 'in exchange for something else'.

The 8 January 1986 ANC policy statement, delivered by Oliver Tambo, contained a veiled message to Mandela: 'Our strength lies in our unity. We must guard that unity like the apple of our eye.' The ANC called for a grand alliance against apartheid incorporating businesspeople, whites, Afrikaners and opinion makers to force government to the negotiating table by 1990. Their deadline proved astonishingly prescient. By 1987, Mandela had sent clandestine messages to the ANC giving notes on talks with government.

PAGES 80 AND 81: A protest march in 1986 demanding the release of imprisoned ANC leaders – Nelson Mandela, Walter Sisulu, Ahmed Kathrada, Govan Mbeki and Raymond Mhlaba – and all other political prisoners.

OPPOSITE: United States senator Jesse Jackson embraces Oliver Tambo during an anti-apartheid demonstration in London in 1985.

The struggle is really not about Mandela, it is about other issues.

JOE SLOVO
SPECIAL MEETING OF THE NATIONAL
WORKING COMMITTEE OF THE ANC,
LUSAKA, 15 OCTOBER 1989

While the ANC declared 1987 the 'Year of the Advance to People's Power', it was skeptical about Mandela's talks. In a highly confidential memo from its National Executive Committee (NEC) meeting (5–9 October 1987), it noted it would consider its position on negotiations, and would brief the ANC membership, the Mass Democratic Movement (the successor to the then banned United Democratic Front), the frontline states and all socialist countries.

The ANC was aware that there was a different feeling in the air: some business groups were circuitously trying to sound others out about the ANC, and others made direct contact. Tambo said in 1989: 'We have said the regime should create a climate for negotiations by releasing Nelson Mandela. If they do we can say that it does demonstrate, in part, a willingness. The British have said the regime cannot hope to negotiate unless Nelson Mandela is released and the ban on the ANC is lifted. The regime will not hurry to lift the ban... . The armed struggle would have to be stepped up even before Nelson Mandela goes out, so that there is no question of his release being conditional on renouncing armed struggle or that the armed struggle will be abandoned because he is out... .' But the ANC was not yet ready for the vision of Mandela, or his belief that only by healing rifts with one's enemies could peace be forged. As a result of the ANC's three decades of exile, paranoia often clouded its judgements.

Not long after this, Tambo became very ill and was sent to London where his family lived. At a meeting of the ANC's National Working Committee (NWC) on 15 August 1989, Alfred Nzo, then Secretary General, said: 'The doctors made a categoric statement that ORT [Tambo] has not suffered a stroke. They said a brief spasm in the vein had momentarily denied the brain oxygen and his condition was owing to that. But they said his nervous reactions were not normal. Generally they were satisfied OR's condition was not very serious.' This was not an accurate summation of Tambo's true condition, and he never fully recovered.

Events were proceeding rapidly. Earlier in 1989, PW Botha had suffered a mild stroke. He was facing increasing resistance from his colleagues for his autocratic style. By the time of the August meeting of the NWC, news had filtered through of PW Botha's resignation. This, with news of an election to be held in September in South Africa, led Steve Tshwete, a member of the ANC's National Executive Committee, to '... express the view that the mere announcement that PW Botha has resigned should not impel us to discuss the internal situation'.

Communist Party deputy chief Joe Slovo countered: 'The NWC has devoted 88 percent of its time to discussing negotiation manoeuvres ... a style is creeping in where we allow international events to influence the working of this NWC.' Although the time to govern was nearing, many ANC leaders did not seem to recognize the import of what was happening.

Mandela was keeping the ANC as fully briefed as he could from prison, but distance and lack of first-hand information about him meant that not everyone was giving his missives the attention they deserved. With Mandela's old friend Oliver Tambo ill in a Stockholm clinic, a curious inertia began to grip the organization and key leaders like Thabo Mbeki were rarely in the frontline states. The ANC began to be propelled by the Mass Democratic Movement (MDM) within South Africa, even though that organization was battling to remain cohesive.

The month after FW de Klerk was voted into office (*see page 79*), the 16 October NEC meeting in Lusaka noted that cleric and MDM leader Alan Boesak '... had called for the regime to be given 6 months and if nothing happened, for an intensification of sanctions'. This was a crucial call that drove the South African government to move faster. A scant four months after Boesak's call De Klerk had agreed to lift restrictions on banned organizations and individuals and free Nelson Mandela.

MK leader Chris Hani was of the opinion that 'The question of NM's [Mandela's] release ought to be taken out of De Klerk's hands ... there should be a lot of organization for a march on Victor Verster to demand the unconditional release of NM. The question of achieving results is important and rural organizations such as Inyadza, Contralesa, should be harnessed.' The ANC was concerned that if De Klerk introduced radical reforms, such as unbanning organizations and releasing Mandela, it would give him credibility and lead to a world prepared to accept a watered-down liberation for South Africa's black people. But they had underestimated international determination for a real transfer of power in South Africa and the wash of optimism and determination that would sweep across South Africa with Mandela's release, making any political solution short of true liberation an exercise in redundancy.

Joe Slovo, Chris Hani and Joe Modise, leaders of Umkhonto we Sizwe in exile, celebrate the ANC's 75th anniversary, Lusaka, Zambia, 8 January 1987.

There was another factor implicit in Hani's comments: over the years the ANC had shifted its focus to urban areas, but the ongoing violence in the then Natal had made it realize the importance of mobilization in rural areas. As would become apparent during bloody township battles in the 1990s, destabilization in the rural areas could quickly lead to uncontrollable acts of bloodshed in urban areas. Slovo cautioned: 'We have had in our history a civic guard movement which the regime used for its purposes. Unless we have the capacity to control such organs, they get out of hand.'

His words were prophetic. Some three years later, when violence was gripping East Rand townships and KwaZulu-Natal, the ANC began training and arming township youth into what it called self-defence units. While many of these units did in fact protect the citizens, most got out of hand terrorizing communities, waging war on opponents – whether political or township feuds – and many became involved in organized criminal activity.

By 1989 repression was so entrenched the ANC was concerned that they would lose the many gains of the 1980s as activists became exhausted, their ranks depleted by jailings and police murders. Early in January 1989, Thabo Mbeki reported after meeting Mass Democratic Movement leaders Murphy Morobe and Mohammed Valli Moosa that '... the UDF [United Democratic Front] is banned ... the leadership of the UDF is characterized by immobility. Murphy Morobe describes it by saying it is as if they are stunned... . There is a broad leadership in the country which has an ANC orientation, but they act within narrow perimeters.'

The ANC often had time to reflect on its shortcomings in the years to come, but it did not always have the time to resolve them. It continued to relegate the opinions of Mandela to a subsidiary level. At a special meeting of the NWC on 15 October 1989 in Lusaka, Joe Slovo reported he had seen the MDM leader Sydney Mufamadi in London: 'He reported that when the MDM heard the release [of eight Rivonia Trialists including Walter Sisulu] was about to happen and that NM wanted to see a delegation they suspected he wanted to counsel a low key reception. The MDM opposed this. NM proceeded to give them a detailed picture of the negotiations that had been going on. He dealt with the history of the releases, how he had negotiated the release of Harry Gwala and Govan Mbeki. He had been critical that they [Gwala and Mbeki] had not been low key and HG's [Gwala's] pictures addressing meetings in an agitated mood had been shown to him. He had not raised his own position, but said the undertaking with the regime was that they play it low key. He said he had seen all seven before their removal [from prison] and they had agreed to play a low key. Sydney said the delegation had come back surprised but they did not hammer the need for the leaders to stand at the head of the mobilization campaign.

'We discussed this [report] in London – about six of us including Ronnie Kasrils, Aziz Pahad, Gertrude Shope and Thabo Mbeki – in short the feeling was that the correct thing was for them [the released leaders] to take their place at the head of the struggle... . We said they must not be low key.' But, in fact, that is exactly the approach the released leaders took. They obeyed Mandela's directive and did nothing to jeopardize the delicate process.

Slovo continued, 'We felt it would be a tragedy if the momentum, the greatest generated in recent history could be deflated. The struggle is really not about Mandela, it is about other issues. He will be released not because of his own recognizances, but because of the ANC.' Slovo's views, in a sense, echoed those of Mandela, who never saw himself as anything other than a disciplined member of a movement of millions, as he made clear in a letter written to PW Botha shortly before he had tea with him at Tuynhuys (*see also* page 79), when Mandela

see also page 79

OPPOSITE: *Archbishop Desmond Tutu leads a service in Soweto, Johannesburg, in May 1988, marking the end of a two-day convocation attended by church leaders from various denominations to discuss non-violent action against apartheid.*

There are four things you have to learn as a prisoner. First, there are the walls. You can see the walls and forever be a prisoner, or you can break through and have the whole world before you in your mind. The second is the warders. Some were very harsh. The third challenge is your friends and comrades. Some people you were very close to outside are impossible to live with in prison. And the fourth, and greatest, challenge is yourself. The enemy within. You have to work with and change yourself.

TOKYO SEXWALE
(FORMER ROBBEN ISLAND PRISONER AND FIRST PREMIER OF GAUTENG)

The path to power

first saw the offices that he would occupy less than a decade later. In the 10-page letter, Mandela wrote to Botha: 'I now consider it necessary in the national interest for the African National Congress and the government to meet urgently to negotiate an effective political settlement.

'At the outset I must point out that I make this move without consultation with the ANC. I must stress that no prisoner, irrespective of his status or influence, can conduct negotiations of this nature from prison ... the question of my release from prison is not an issue, at least at this stage of the discussions... . A government which used violence against blacks many years before we took up arms has no right whatsoever to call on us to lay down arms... . No dedicated ANC member will

Well-wishers outside Tygerberg Hospital, Cape Town, where Mandela was recovering from tuberculosis in 1988.

ever heed a call to break with the SACP. We regard such a demand as a purely divisive government strategy. It is a call on us to commit suicide. ...

'Two central issues will have to be addressed at such a meeting: firstly, the demand for majority rule in a unitary state; secondly, the concern of white South Africa over this demand, as well as the insistence of whites on structural guarantees that majority rule will not mean domination of the white minority by blacks.'

In 1989 the ANC found events were moving faster than it could monitor them, and certainly control was out of the question. The ANC had planned that '... in the build up to or after the release [of Mandela] there should be systematic effective actions of MK to create the necessary atmosphere for action. These actions should strictly be directed at targets in keeping with movement policy and should be accompanied by propaganda with slogans such as: Welcome home dear commander. None of these operations should be conducted in or close to areas where NM would be at any particular moment.' However, because De Klerk did not give forewarning of his decision, and because ANC management was so chaotic at that time, these plans came to nought. Political change would develop its own momentum.

The unbanning of the ANC and the release of Nelson Mandela found the ANC in the eye of what seemed like a hurricane. The world's media, which had been beating a regular path to its door since 1988, now descended upon Lusaka en masse. Umkhonto we Sizwe soldiers, who dreamed they would march down the highways of Pretoria and Johannesburg in military battalions, atop tanks, with crowds cheering and streamers flying, like the images they had seen on old Soviet newsreels, instead returned to a situation none had considered: a negotiated peace. They could find no work. Like Vietnam veterans two decades before who had suffered acute trauma and psychological anguish at being returned into societies which not only did not cheer their return, but were embarrassed by their role as combatants, many former liberation army soldiers turned to drink, drugs, suicide and crime.

Within hours of his release, Mandela proved himself the greatest of all ANC leaders. At his first press conference at Bishopscourt the day after his release the South African press corps, many skeptical whether he would make the grade, gave him a standing ovation. He displayed a warmth and an intellect that astonished and impressed all.

On the day of his release, 11 February 1990, Mandela made it clear that he was an obedient cadre of the ANC: 'I intend making only a few preliminary comments at this stage. ... Mr de Klerk ... is a man of integrity who is acutely aware of the dangers of a public figure not honouring his undertakings.' He tried to allay white fears, and condemned the crime that terrorized people, regardless of skin colour.

At the Soweto rally on 13 February, he told the enormous crowd sweltering in the heat: 'As proud as I am of the Soweto community I have been greatly disturbed by the statistics of crime I have read in the newspapers. Although I understand the deprivations our people suffer, I must make it clear that the level of crime in our township is unhealthy and must be eliminated as a matter of urgency... . I stated in 1964 that I and the ANC are as opposed to black domination as we are to white domination. We must accept, however, that our statements and declarations alone will not be sufficient to allay the fears of white South Africans. We must clearly demonstrate our goodwill to our white compatriots and convince them by our conduct and argument that a South Africa without apartheid will be a better home for all.'

Mandela re-entered the ANC quietly but firmly. At his first meetings with the ANC in Lusaka shortly after his release, he stood with dignity towering over most of his comrades. He listened more than he spoke at those early meetings, but when he spoke it was with an unshakeable authority that deterred skeptics from questioning too strongly, and he remained a powerful force in every ANC meeting he would chair. He would not tolerate thoughtlessness, or rhetoric for the sake of cliché-ridden words: he wanted considered thinking, and if he heard thought-out views he would listen intently, his hands clasped in front of him, and comment only at the end of the discourse. Foolish, shallow thoughts, however, could expect a sharp rebuke. By these means he disciplined his followers to sharpen their focus, improve their information, work harder and strategize more carefully.

The dichotomy between a revolutionary ANC planning to overthrow government and an ANC preparing to govern soon became

A crowd defies armed troops present during a mass funeral, Alexandria, Eastern Cape, during the mid-1980s.

As the representatives of
centuries of white minority
rule bowed to the results of
the democratic process, the
people did, as Martin
Luther King Jr did, cry out:
Free at last, free at last,
thank God Almighty, we
are free at last!

NELSON MANDELA
ADDRESSING THE JOINT HOUSES
OF THE CONGRESS OF THE USA,
6 OCTOBER 1994

RIGHT: *A defiant Nelson
Mandela in Cape Town in the
garden of Archbishop Desmond
Tutu's Bishopscourt house on
12 February 1990, the day after
his release from prison.*

OPPOSITE: *Jubilant Soweto
citizens celebrate the release of
Nelson Mandela.*

apparent. As early as 1990 it was noting its concern that there was '... confusion between ANC, Sayco [SA Youth Congress], UDF etc. All go to different areas and do not act in concert. ANC talks of uniting all forces, and chiefs may be present. The next body comes along and says down with chiefs. We are to blame. We told the youth to make the country ungovernable, but the situation has changed. Our strategy has changed from saying down with everything, to organizing the chiefs to be on our side. ... We have not gone to organizations and structures to explain the new strategies. We have to stop conflicting statements and positions.'

In June 1991 the ANC had its first national conference at home. Hundreds of delegates met at the University of Durban-Westville. They had lunch on the steps of the university, eating *pap* and *vleis* (maize porridge and meat) off polystyrene plates. They exchanged stories of the struggle at home, and of the difficulties of life in exile. Exile and internal South African activist looked at each other and embraced. Nelson Mandela had brought his people home; now they had to settle down to negotiate a democratic future for all.

Crafting a negotiating table

Walk through the door and take your place at the negotiating table together with the government. The time for negotiation has arrived.

PRESIDENT FW DE KLERK
2 FEBRUARY 1990

Frederick de Klerk did not ask Mandela to give up violence when he released him on 11 February 1990, as PW Botha had when Mandela's release was discussed (*see* page 73). De Klerk's government had little intention of giving up violence. Death squads were still operating and detentions continued. The chemical and biological warfare programme was operating at full speed despite South Africa's signing international treaties in 1974 that it would not develop a chemical warfare capacity.

The head of South Africa's Defence Force Special Operations, Brigadier Wouter Basson, had just purchased 500 kilograms of the essential agent for mandrax (a stable seller among Cape Flats gangsters) from Croatia. Perhaps the ingredient was not intended for the manufacture of a teargas, as Basson's staff told the Truth and Reconciliation Commission (TRC) in 1998. TRC commissioners were seeking to establish whether South Africa's operators of its chemical and biological warfare programme had become a major drugs supplier to South Africa's black youth. This may explain why, when African National Congress activists tried to hold meetings or canvas support in the Cape Flats areas, they were intimidated and forced out by drug lords.

The question of Nelson Mandela's release ought to be taken out of De Klerk's hands.

CHRIS HANI
ANC NATIONAL EXECUTIVE COMMITTEE
MEETING MINUTES, 26 OCTOBER 1989

PAGES 92 AND 93: Cyril Ramaphosa, Nelson Mandela and Joe Slovo during a 1992 march to commemorate the 1976 Soweto student uprising.

While De Klerk stunned the world by removing restrictions from banned organizations and releasing Nelson Mandela, his government clearly believed they could control the situation. A primary aim seemed to be to prise open the jaws of the sanctions that were biting deep into the economy. Govan Mbeki said: 'This was a war without absolute winners. African nationalism and Afrikaner nationalism, the two major political forces in South Africa, had fought to a draw... . Negotiations were the only option left to arrive at a settlement that would encompass all the people of South Africa. And so it happened that the oppressor and the oppressed came together to chart the road to a democratic South Africa.'

De Klerk had promised a '... new South Africa, a totally changed South Africa' upon his election in September 1989. His office began quietly confiding in journalists and diplomats that the opening of parliament the following year would reveal dramatic reforms. Visas for foreign journalists, usually difficult to obtain, became freely available. But the foreign press and diplomatic corps had been bitten once before by a South African government that had promised reforms: PW Botha did the same in 1985 before his disastrous Rubicon speech, where he not only gave no reforms but launched an arrogant diatribe against the world.

Is it politically correct to continue preaching peace and non-violence when dealing with a government whose barbaric practices have brought so much suffering and misery to Africans?

NELSON MANDELA
(SECRETARY OF THE NATIONAL
ACTION COUNCIL OF SOUTH AFRICA)
REVIEW OF 29, 30, 31 MAY
GENERAL STRIKE, 1961

A rally held in Soweto to welcome home the seven ANC leaders, among them Walter Sisulu, Elias Motsoaledi and Wilton Mkwayi, who were released on 15 October 1989.

Crafting a negotiating table

There was little to suggest that conservative De Klerk, who had imposed restrictive legislation against universities when he was Minister of Education, had had a Damascene conversion. De Klerk, a devout man, belonged to the same Reformed Church that had provided the theological basis to apartheid in the late 1930s. Dominee Pieter Dumans had been expelled by the ruling church ring in December 1987, allegedly for breaking the fifth commandment, 'Honour thy father and mother', and the ninth, 'Thou shalt not bear false witness', after he swore in a coloured man as the church's first elder. In July 1988, Dumans was reinstated after approaching the Supreme Court for a decision. Even on readmission to the church, he was forbidden from administering sacraments or from ministering to his congregation. Did De Klerk, as a devout follower of a church with such strict dictates, have the courage to bring about reforms? It seemed unlikely, but what was certain was that the nation was exhausted by apartheid, sanctions and a decade of harsh repression.

On 13 September 1989, the day before his installation as President, in an astounding reversal, De Klerk gave permission for 20,000 anti-apartheid activists to march in Cape Town.

Early in October, Thabo Mbeki, Jacob Zuma, Steve Tshwete and a few others who formed the President's Committee held one of a series of meetings with the Broederbond, the ideological wing of the National Party and Afrikanerdom. In a sense these meetings were the first real negotiating platforms between the ANC in exile and the Broederbond. On 9 October, Thabo Mbeki, reporting back to the National Executive Committee (NEC) about that meeting, said the Broederbond had informed them that the release of key political prisoners was to begin, but that Mandela would be the last to be released. The minutes note Mbeki reported, 'The broeders identified obstacles to change as follows: The National Party does not want to lose control of the pace of change; Fear of black domination; De Klerk's desire to restructure the state machinery because he does not like the State Security Council; Mistrust of the ANC. Regime not happy with the idea that the Harare OAU [Organization of African Unity] declaration be tabled to the UN which will make it mandatory. It was explained to them that the intervention of the international community will be a matter of negotiation.'

On 15 October De Klerk released all the remaining Rivonia Trialists with the exception of Mandela. On 16 November, he scrapped the Separate Amenities Act, but this was too much for some right-wing communities. In Bethal in the province now called Mpumalanga, town fathers filled the town swimming pool with soil to prevent black people swimming in it. At Ermelo, no more than 100 kilometres north-east of Bethal, a man with a *sjambok* (a plastic whip) beat up three black children who dared swim in the town's swimming pool with white children. A horrified white mother videotaped the incident and it became an international news story.

The ANC was left somewhat off-balance by all this change, which was moving faster than foreseen. In a discussion document, 'Unbanning of ANC, Some strategic considerations', it noted that it should rapidly try to build its military wing, but without forming a threatening presence that could cause De Klerk to backtrack and the ANC to lose face. It also began its first real plan to construct itself as a legitimate organization. It began tussling with the issues surrounding the return of exiles: the guarantees it would need for their safety, their resettlement and even the issue of identity documents.

On the morning of 2 February 1990, offices all around South Africa stopped work as employees crowded around radios and television sets to hear the news all believed would change their lives. And it came. De Klerk said in parliament: 'The time has come to break out of the cycle of violence and break through to peace and reconciliation. The silent majority is yearning for this.' He then scrolled through a litany of organizations the government was unbanning, and a list of repressive legislation it was sweeping aside. He told a hushed parliament that no final date had been set for Mandela's release but he wanted to '... bring the matter to finality without delay.' However, he endorsed his party's commitment to privatization – at the time the ANC was committed to nationalization.

Some South Africans wept before their television sets with relief and joy. Others sent for champagne which they drank in their offices. Still others sat in huddled circles, trying to evaluate what this would mean to their lives. Share prices soared on the Johannesburg Stock Exchange. A protest march outside parliament evaporated after the news. Anglican Archbishop Desmond Tutu said he had to give credit to De Klerk for this step. The ANC leadership, which was visiting the ailing Oliver Tambo in his Stockholm clinic (*see* page 84), was surly and barely commented. The Mass Democratic Movement (MDM) said the reforms were 'progressive' and welcomed the 'boldness of some of the steps.' That night, parties were held across the country.

The time has come to break out of the cycle of violence and break through to peace and reconciliation. The silent majority is yearning for this.

PRESIDENT FW DE KLERK
2 FEBRUARY 1990

The ANC learnt with dismay of the guilty verdicts and lengthy sentences imposed on comrade Winnie Mandela and her codefendants today 14 May 1991. As leave to appeal both the verdicts and the sentences has been granted, the matter is sub-judice. The last word on this entire affair has not yet been spoken. We elect to leave the matter in the hands of the courts, fully confident that in the end the truth will emerge.

PRESS RELEASE, ANC DEPARTMENT OF
INFORMATION AND PUBLICITY

Cyril Ramaphosa, Secretary General of the National Union of Mineworkers and an MDM leader, was recuperating from pneumonia in a Johannesburg clinic. On a telephone in his private ward, he began urgent consultations with Mohammed Valli Moosa, Sydney Mufamadi, Murphy Morobe and other MDM leaders. A plane was chartered and put on standby for them to fly to Cape Town for Mandela's imminent release. Everyone associated with the ANC was preparing for power, and hoping not to repeat the mistakes of the past.

Nelson Mandela walks to freedom from Victor Verster prison on 11 Februrary 1990 with his wife Winnie.

This was a war without absolute winners. African nationalism and Afrikaner nationalism, the two major political forces in South Africa, fought to a draw. Negotiations were the only option left to arrive at a settlement that would encompass all the people of South Africa. And so it happened that the oppressor and the oppressed came together to chart the road to a democratic South Africa.

GOVAN MBEKI
SUNSET AT MIDDAY, 1996

On 11 February, Nelson Mandela walked out of the gates of Victor Verster prison in Paarl, hand-in-hand with his wife Winnie. That evening he read a carefully crafted, dull speech from Cape Town's Grand Parade. US senator Jesse Jackson ripped his suit climbing a fence in an unsuccessful attempt to be near Mandela. Ramaphosa checked out of hospital to be present and, with a plaster marking the spot where the drip had been removed from his hand, held Mandela's microphone and put himself between Madiba and an enthusiastic crowd.

Walter Sisulu, Nelson Mandela and Cyril Ramaphosa during Mandela's first public address in 27 years, at Cape Town's Grand Parade, 11 February 1990. He wore Winnie's spectacles, having forgotten his own at Victor Verster prison.

The Nelson Mandela Homecoming Committee had meant him to go home to Soweto that night, but events in Cape Town were more chaotic than any could have anticipated. Archbishop Tutu was at the Cape Town City Hall when organizers told him Mandela would stay at his home in elite Bishopscourt that night. 'He was concerned that if he was staying in Cape Town it should not be in a white area, but his security detail were concerned that they would not be able to control a township situation. Trevor Manuel and Dullah Omar convinced Mandela that I had transformed Bishopscourt into a people's place. We did not have much of an exchange with him that night. When he arrived he immediately went into a meeting. Walter Sisulu and most of the leadership were there, but what we did do once they had all gathered was to pray. We also said the Lord's Prayer and sang a Xhosa hymn, "Masibulele Kayesu" (Let us say Thank You Jesus). But he was not allowed to have an uninterrupted meeting. He kept getting calls, we'd answer the phone and people would say, "This is the White House", "This is President Kaunda." My wife Leah was in Soweto, but I was helped by staff and friends. We coped. My physician, Ingrid le Roux, is a Swedish doctor, and she was the first doctor to see him in freedom, something she cherishes very much.'

Mandela's long walk to freedom had ended; now the steep climb to democracy began. Reflecting on those difficult early negotiation days, and on Mandela as a leader and a person, Mac Maharaj, a key ANC strategist and Transport Minister in Mandela's government, said it was important to '... focus on the humanism of a man whose life is inseparable from our organization. The great men and women who stand out in history have all been driven by the need to remove suffering and injustice. What is startling about them is that, although most of them have suffered, they transcend bitterness about their own personal misfortunes. They are moved by the suffering of others. Their own suffering is submerged in their quest for a better world. The only time we have seen a glimpse inside Nelson Mandela is when he reflects on his own family. Then you see his pain and the anguish – and even so it is about his self beyond himself. But betray him or his cause, and Madiba turns to icy steel. De Klerk learnt this lesson the hard way when he failed to stop the violence in the early 1990s. From being described by Madiba on his release as "a man of integrity", De Klerk later withered in every public encounter with Mandela. ... Just as democracy could not have been achieved without an organized political force, so too is the realization of transformation of our country impossible without the ANC leading the process. The struggle to bring about such fundamental changes has always been accompanied by another very different struggle – that of making the ANC the effective instrument it needs to be. This parallel "struggle" is a very different one conducted on a very different terrain and with different rules. But there are many lessons from our past with great relevance for the present challenges we face.'

I stand here before you, not as a prophet, but as a humble servant of you, the people.

Confronting the reality of endemic violence in South Africa horrified the returning ANC members. It was one thing discussing violence and watching it on foreign news, but the intensity of violence in KwaZulu-Natal and the townships flanking Johannesburg shocked them. The cordial backslapping of the Groote Schuur Minute, when key members of the ANC National Executive Committee met with government, was soon replaced with helpless horror.

The Groote Schuur Minute of May 1990 established a working group to make recommendations on the definition of a political offence, as well as devising the norms and mechanisms for the release of political prisoners and granting of immunity. It noted: 'Temporary immunity from prosecution for political offences committed before today will be considered on an urgent basis for members of the NEC and selected other members of the ANC from outside the country to enable them to return and help with the establishment and management of political activities to assist in bringing violence to an end.'

The ANC delegation, consisting of seven black and two white people and one coloured and one Indian person (nine men and two women), was selected not only because of the delegates' capabilities but also to make a statement about racial equality and gender sensitivity. The government delegation was nine men, all white, all Afrikaner. The ANC demanded 20,000 to 40,000 exiles be allowed to return home. In the minutes of the ANC NWC of 11 May 1990, the belief was recorded that the 'De Klerk delegation appeared determined to achieve progress. Regarding the armed struggle De Klerk said that rhetoric encourages street violence.'

The ANC had no infrastructure. It operated out of offices which it was loaned in the Munich Re building opposite the offices of *The Star* newspaper in downtown Johannesburg. Sympathizers loaned computers, fax machines, cars, even their services.

The ANC delegation to the Groote Schuur Minute of May 1990: (front row from left) Ruth Mompati, Alfred Nzo, Nelson Mandela, Joe Slovo, Walter Sisulu and Cheryl Carolus; (back row from left) Archie Gumede, Ahmed Kathrada, Joe Modise, Beyers Naudé and Thabo Mbeki.

In late July police uncovered Operation Vula ('the opening') which had been set up in 1988 as a network of ultra-secret Umkhonto we Sizwe cells. De Klerk was furious and the securocrats in his establishment tried to persuade him to cut off talks. But he was angry, not stupid: he had begun a process that had to continue.

The next round of top level talks took place the following month. The Pretoria Minute was signed at the Presidency in Pretoria on 6 August 1990. The final report, dated 21 May 1990, of the working group on political offences was accepted. The meeting instructed the working group to draw up a plan for the release of ANC prisoners and the granting of indemnity in a phased manner and to report before the end of August. The further release of prisoners was set to begin on 1 September 1990. Indemnities would begin from 1 October 1990, and be complete before the end of the year, to enable the return of exiles. These were all wishful deadlines. Talks embraced a labyrinth of operational details, bureaucracies to be waded through, and even humane considerations, such as pre-release counselling for prisoners and housing exiles, that made those first deadlines impossible to fulfil.

The most important and controversial announcement was that the ANC would '... suspend all armed actions with immediate effect. No further armed actions and related activities by the ANC and its military wing Umkhonto we Sizwe will take place.' Both delegations expressed serious concern about the general level of violence, intimidation and unrest in the country, especially in the then province of Natal. They agreed that it was vital that understanding should grow among all sections of the South African population '... that problems can and should be solved through negotiations'. Both of the parties committed themselves to undertake measures '... to promote and expedite the normalization and stabilization of the situation in line with the spirit of mutual trust obtaining among the leaders involved'. Government undertook to lift the State of Emergency in Natal and to begin repealing security legislation. The Pretoria Minute concluded on an upbeat note, that was unfortunately not to last: 'We are convinced that what we have agreed upon today can become a milestone on the road to true peace and prosperity for our country. All of us can henceforth walk that road in consul-

Both delegations [of the ANC and government] agreed that it was vital that understanding should grow among all sections of the South African population, that problems can and should be solved through negotiations.

THE PRETORIA MINUTE SIGNED BY THE NATIONAL PARTY GOVERNMENT AND THE ANC, PRETORIA, 6 AUGUST 1990

tation and cooperation with each other. We call upon all those who have not yet committed themselves to peaceful negotiations to do so now. The way is now open to proceed toward negotiations on a new constitution.'

Violence, however, was spiralling out of control. Armed groups attacked people on trains, spraying them with automatic gunfire and throwing them onto railway tracks. Years later at TRC hearings it would be revealed that these were government death squads. De Klerk denied knowledge of these events at TRC hearings, but enough overall evidence came out to suggest that, although he might not have known of each and every incident of the hundreds, or even thousands, that occurred, he certainly knew of some.

Mandela, faced with media coverage of people being hacked with pangas and of police massacres, was beginning to boil with anger. The minutes of the ANC National Executive Committee of 12 and 13 September 1990 show that, seven months after government had

The huge East Rand squatter camp of Phola Park was formed after people fled violence in nearby Zonke'sizwe and were joined by displaced people from other areas. In 1990 incendiary bombs were used to burn down part of the squatter camp. Residents accused police of complicity with Inkatha in this attack.

'Usuthu, usuthu.' This deep chant from approaching Zulu impis terrified every township resident in Gauteng in the early 1990s, as terrible clashes daily claimed the lives of dozens. This impi from Vosloorus on the East Rand prepares for battle.

unbanned the ANC and long before the return of exiles or major releases of political prisoners, the ANC was already thinking of suspending negotiations. The minutes read, 'Reports on the violence indicate the deep involvement of the police with Inkatha. Residents reported that in Phola Park incendiary bombs were used to burn down the squatter camp. Police wearing balaclavas had accompanied those wearing red bands. Threats were made against those sheltering refugees... . People accused the ANC of doing nothing to protect them. People were publicly tearing up their membership cards. There was the fear that unless we took the initiative, police would begin arming both sides leading to an escalation in conflict. It was said the people would defend themselves but in a way that is ill disciplined, revenge seeking and not as effective unless we deploy trained people to assist and establish a framework within which such self-defence should take place. This must not be done in secret.'

There was an appeal for a central body of self-defence units but these too became uncontrollable. The minutes noted 'extensive discussion was held on the recommendation by the deputy president [Mandela] that we suspend the talks. It was agreed that an extraordinarily extended NEC meeting be called to consider the suspension of talks with the regime. The time has come for us to tell De Klerk that he settles the issue of violence within seven days or talks are suspended.' A few days later, 18 September 1990, Mandela called an emergency extended session of the NEC where he detailed what had taken place at a bitter meeting between him and De Klerk. Mandela said he had questioned police involvement in killings. He told the

NEC De Klerk had denied this, saying Mandela said that '... the security forces were behind them on peace initiatives.' Mandela said he pointed out to De Klerk that there had been 4,000 deaths in Natal and 700 in the townships flanking Johannesburg, with pitifully few arrests and no signs of violence abating. De Klerk responded: 'There is a third force orchestrating the violence and government has taken the decision to weed out those elements'. General Constand Viljoen, who was head of the army, chipped in, 'There is no third force in the sense of an independent organization but there are mischievous elements.'

Mandela challenged the readiness with which the security forces opened fire on township residents. He opposed government's intended erection of razor wire around hostels inhabited by rural workers to the cities and towns, even though publicly the ANC was calling for this. He pointed out that some hostels were already fenced, '... but police have allowed armed troublemakers to come out.'

Mandela said that he, Penuell Maduna, Zola Skweyiya and Matthews Phosa had met with police commissioner General Johan Coetzee, a General van Heerden and Tim McNally, the attorney general of the then Natal, to push for arrests and convictions. But to little avail. The NEC meeting became heated as ANC Natal leader Harry Gwala launched into a spluttering diatribe: 'People in Natal are now living in the bush, they are being hunted down. The choice is either they join Inkatha or face death. The police are visiting locations and telling people they have no need of arms since ANC has stopped armed struggle. People are calling on the ANC to enable them to defend themselves.' Mandela replied, 'What response can we give to that request?' None had an answer. Mandela mused, 'What we need is pressure to stop government duplicity.'

Anger within the tripartite alliance of the ANC, the Congress of South African Trade Unions (Cosatu) and the South African Communist Party (SACP) was intense. All had family or friends who had had to flee their homes, or who had been killed or injured in violence. At a tripartite alliance meeting later that month the decision taken on 6 August to suspend the armed struggle was attacked. Mandela found his motives being questioned and brought into disrepute among his own people. A comment at the meeting summed it up: 'We operate as though it is possible to enter into gentleman's agreements with the regime.' Some pressed for international mediation, while others said: 'We must stipulate deadlines linked to mass action.'

Mandela began responding in language which De Klerk understood better than pleas. On 11 December he wrote to the heads of government attending the European Community Summit to request that decisions on sanctions be postponed until early 1991. 'Despite all our efforts we have as yet not succeeded in removing the obstacles to negotiations as visualized in the UN General Assembly Declaration [which was essentially the Harare Declaration] on South Africa adopted last December. The overwhelming majority of political prisoners have as yet not been released and people continue to be detained without trial, to mention only two obstacles. The important agreement we reached with the government on the 6th of August to begin exploratory talks on constitutional matters has not yet been implemented, owing to the refusal of the government to begin these talks.'

Mandela came under attack and was questioned about his personal relationship with De Klerk and his frequently quoted position that De Klerk was a man of integrity. The African National Congress and the National Party and, most of all, the people of South Africa, were going to have to prove their commitment to peace over and over again through numerous trials. And now the mettle and leadership of Nelson Mandela would be tried as never before.

The only time we have a glimpse inside Nelson Mandela is when he reflects on his own family. Then you see his pain and the anguish – and even so it is about his self beyond himself. But betray him or his cause, and Madiba turns to icy steel. De Klerk learnt this lesson the hard way when he failed to stop the violence in the early 1990s. From being described by Madiba on his release as 'a man of integrity', De Klerk later withered in every public encounter with Mandela.

MAC MAHARAJ
(FORMER ROBBEN ISLANDER AND MINISTER OF TRANSPORT), 1998

A clash of values

Take your guns, your knives and your pangas and throw them into the sea. Close down the death factories. End this war now!

NELSON MANDELA
SPEECH IN DURBAN, 25 FEBRUARY 1990

Before he left prison, Nelson Mandela wrote to his old friend Mangosuthu Gatsha Buthelezi, the leader of the Zulu-based Inkatha Freedom Party (IFP), appealing for his help in ending the civil war in KwaZulu-Natal. More than 15,000 people had died in conflict that had raged for five years by the time of Mandela's release in 1990. Well over a million had been made homeless, refugees in the land of their birth.

Mandela and Buthelezi were introduced by Walter Sisulu in the 1950s. For many years, with the African National Congress (ANC) banned and in exile and some of its leaders in jail, Buthelezi carried on many ANC traditions. In 1975, Buthelezi, encouraged by the ANC, launched Inkatha, a Zulu cultural organization that quickly developed a political face. Inkatha even adopted the ANC's black, green and gold colours. By 1979, opinion polls showed he was even more popular than Mandela among black people. However, tensions had begun developing between him and the ANC and, by 1979, they had widened into a chasm of mistrust.

Mandela and Buthelezi only finally, publicly, met almost a year after Mandela's release. In the interim Mandela appealed to the youth ('the shock troops of the struggle', as he called them) to show greater understanding toward homeland leaders like Buthelezi. Addressing the South African Youth Congress on 13 April 1990 at KaNyamazane in KaNgwane, Mandela urged: 'I want to appeal to you, not to be unnecessarily hostile against the homeland leaders. These men are our flesh and blood and we want them to join the struggle. We know some went into this system honestly thinking it was an effective option. But those who have discovered their mistakes and are prepared to come to the liberation movement let us welcome them with open arms. There is no need to say because a man has made a mistake before, we should no longer work with him – we must welcome them.'

Buthelezi had in fact been anticipating a meeting with the ANC since 1989. The ANC's National Working Committee in Lusaka on 7 August 1989, attended by Alfred Nzo, Joe Slovo, Jacob Zuma and others, heard that Buthelezi was delaying a meeting by imposing demands. 'For the summit to take place, he insists President Oliver Tambo should personally invite him... . Meeting agreed we ought to keep a record of correspondence with GB [Buthelezi] to expose [at appropriate time] that GB is intent on torpedoing peace talks.' This comment from the minutes of the meeting underscored a tone that had lasted for long, and would continue.

Old rivalries die hard, particularly if they are being fuelled. A brilliant ANC document circulated to senior officials in April 1991, titled 'Counter Revolution in the Making – Toward a common perception of violence in the transitional period', probably hit the nail on the head when it said: 'Violence in any situation is not an end in itself. It pursues given political objectives.' It suggested that government strategy (as was confirmed later by Truth and Reconciliation hearings) was to 'present itself as a force indispensable to the process of transition both as the manager of the process and the force best placed to secure it'. In other words, violence was a tool that the state would use to underscore their message that black people, in particular the ANC, were incompetent to rule.

But, as violence spiralled over the years, no-one could control it. The huge East Rand squatter camp of Phola Park, which by 1992 had some 45,000 inhabitants, was formed after people fled violence in nearby Zonke'sizwe and were joined, in turn, by displaced people from other areas. In the rutted tracks of the hastily built shantytown, children played mock battles with cardboard shields, sticks for spears and crudely made AK47s, enacting the battles of their parents. Early in the same year 10,000 people disappeared from Folweni near Amanzimtoti, fleeing violence. Another 4,000 fled Umlazi, 1,000 from Murchison.

Entire villages were bereft of inhabitants, doors swinging eerily open, chickens pecking in the dirt, goats and pigs searching for food. In graveyards, mounds of red soil always seemed to be piled next to more newly open graves for victims of the latest massacre. The final TRC report blamed the IFP for 4,000 murders, the ANC for 1,000 and the South African police and KwaZulu police for falling into the next largest categories of those responsible for killings in the region. Buthelezi recalled Mandela's letter written to him from prison: 'Mandela was expressing his anguish and said we should get together because the violence was a shame to us as African leaders. A few days after his release he phoned me to say thank you for his release and wanted me to accompany him to the king [Goodwill Zwelithini] about the violence. I fixed dates for a meeting but it never materialized. It was only much later that he told me radicals like Harry Gwala and others were saying under no circumstances must he meet with me.

'It is a pity, the history of the country would have been quite different. Jointly we may have defused the violence sooner and that would have had its own rewards for us. Later, we

PAGES 106 AND 107: An Inkatha Freedom Party official from Dube hostel in Soweto leads an impi *on a protest march, 16 March 1996.*

ABOVE: Nelson Mandela attends a rally in KwaZulu-Natal with ANC leaders from the area, among them Jeff Radebe and Jacob Zuma, both dressed in full Zulu regalia.

Violence in KwaZulu-Natal kept threatening to torpedo not only transitional negotiations and constitutional talks but the democratic process itself.

went to the Security Council in New York, he described me as a surrogate of the National Party. I'd always placed him on a pedestal when United Democratic Front people and those in exile attacked me. I'd always put him in a class of his own. I was devastated.'

While politicians are able to cause conflict with words, they cannot simply douse it with words. Violence, once begun, develops a life of its own and can be manipulated by other forces, political groupings or criminal elements, to their advantage. The ongoing murders

in townships and rural areas saw conflict emerge between Mandela and President FW de Klerk after a clash between a Zulu *impi* and ANC mourners in July 1990. De Klerk, despite a warning from Mandela that an attack was expected by Inkatha, did nothing to prevent it. The two sides clashed at a funeral in Sebokeng and 32 people died.

Visibly angry, Mandela later told a press conference, 'I said, "You were warned beforehand. You did nothing about it. Why? Why have there been no arrests? In any other country where 32 people had been slaughtered in this way, the head of state would come out condemning the matter and consoling the next of kin. Why have you not done so?".' Mandela said that De Klerk had no answer.

Instead, on 31 August that same year, government enacted changes to the Zulu code in KwaZulu-Natal, that was signed by De Klerk: 'No black shall carry an assegai, wood stick, battle axe, stick shod with iron, staff or sharp-pointed stick or any other dangerous weapon [except] if a person could prove he had the bona fide intention to carry such dangerous weapons in accordance with traditional Zulu usage, customs or religions.' No other ethnic grouping in the country was accorded similar 'cultural' rights. And so for the first time, in the midst of the killing fields of KwaZulu-Natal, these brutal killing implements attained legitimacy.

The ANC, which was recently unbanned and barely functioning within South Africa, was spun into a crisis. The minutes of the ANC National Executive Committee (NEC) special meeting of 12 and 13 September 1990, chaired by Mandela, noted: 'Reports on the violence indicate the deep involvement of the police with Inkatha' (*see also* page 104).

We had to institute transformation in terms of policies, laws and institutions: budgets, civil service and delivery mechanisms all constitute governance. How do you deliver in an innovative and creative way and transform orthodoxy to revolutionary?

JAY NAIDOO (MINISTER OF POSTS, TELECOMMUNICATIONS AND BROADCASTING)

There was an appeal at the NEC for a centrally organized body of self-defence units. These were established but became forces beyond the control of any political leadership.

The NEC noted: 'Buthelezi will not simply be satisfied with a meeting with Mandela. He is working with the government and certain international forces. A meeting that ends in failure will be disastrous and violence will become even worse... . We have made an error in our approach [to government] giving the impression we will not allow anything to stop the negotiating process.'

Mandela was at his wits' end. He had tried to gain public sympathy for homeland leaders like Buthelezi in public pronouncements. He had incurred criticism from ANC members by repeatedly calling De Klerk a man of integrity and Buthelezi his brother. He had even suggested, not long after his release, to the ANC leadership that Buthelezi, De Klerk and he should visit strife-torn areas together, 'to find out what is happening'. The ANC agreed to the suggestion, but neither De Klerk nor Buthelezi could agree. The ANC threatened to suspend negotiations on 4 April 1991, after an NEC meeting where it demanded that De Klerk comply with a list of seven measures to end violence by 9 May.

And yet, only months before this, the IFP and ANC had held warm, thoughtful, but regrettably often secret, meetings. On 26 September 1990, ANC and IFP officials met and reaffirmed the need to 'end the violence immediately'. Within three weeks, they met again. Journalists, sitting outside the briefing room on 15 October 1990, said the meeting seemed relaxed and friendly, and occasional laughter could be heard from the room. However, no press statement was made other than to say talks had been cordial. Behind closed doors, the delegation, consisting of John Nkadimeng, Jacob Zuma, Thabo Mbeki, Joe Nhlanhla, Josiah Jele and Joel Netshitenzhe from the ANC, and Frank Mdlalose, ESE Sithebe, VB Ndlovu, ET Bhengu, M Zondi and N Nkehli from the IFP, had agreed to a meeting between their leaders. It was a shame that they did not feel the need to take the public into their confidence, because the difficulties, recorded in the minutes, give a deeper understanding of the problems – and how trivial were some of the issues that caused war.

The minutes note: 'The main problem within the IFP is that township councillors had not involved other local leaders, particularly the chiefs. These leaders felt left out ... [and] for some people, violence has become a source of revenue; others have emerged as heroes in the violence and it is difficult to sell peace to them.' A further obstacle to peace was, 'Local leaders [from the ANC and IFP] fear being seen in each other's company because this might infuriate their followers. We need local people to get used to solving problems together. This will help resolve problems of unfounded rumours, serve as an example to the people and facilitate the whole process.'

In words that would be echoed over and over again during the next four years, this

Arson, the commonest form of attack in KwaZulu-Natal, saw thousands of people lose their homes.

positive meeting observed, 'Statements from the top can jeopardize local peace initiatives. If one of the leaders makes a hostile statement, the grassroots are bound to identify with the statement and it bedevils the whole process. We appeal to leaders at the highest level to assist the committee by not making statements which could undermine the [peace] process.'

There were a number of very secret meetings between Buthelezi and Mandela too, before their first public meeting on 29 January 1991 in Durban. Despite the public smiles and handshakes, at the latter it was clear to the huge press corps gathered outside that there were serious tensions. Behind closed doors, Mandela told Buthelezi that the '... violence now escalating in the country is an indictment to the black leadership as a whole. This is not the time to apportion blame. We must accept collective responsibility for what is going on. There is an element of faction fighting in what is going on and it is necessary to recognize there is a third force at work.' Buthelezi accepted the existence of such a third force but said it would require deeper discussion at Inkatha central committee level.

The body of an old man who was slain outside his home in Bambayi township, KwaZulu-Natal, in March 1994.

A clash of values

*A funeral service for the
victims of the Boipatong
massacre, 29 June 1992.*

There were also light moments between the ANC and IFP. Suzanne Vos, who is now an IFP parliamentarian, remembered: 'I flew down for a meeting in Durban. There was a picture of me with the wealthy Sandton branch of the IFP in the newspaper, and Mandela said, "I saw your picture in the paper this morning." Then he said, "Do your members take their cultural weapons to the meetings?" I said, "No, my members just rattle their jewels." '

Sadly, these moments of lightness were rare, and a lot more blood was to flow. In July 1991, secret papers were unearthed by newspapers which showed that Inkatha was being funded by government. They also showed that some IFP cadres were being trained in secret military camps by the South African military and were also receiving weapons from them.

Worse was to come. On 17 June 1992, a Zulu *impi* from KwaMadala hostel, flanking Iscor's steel works, crept across darkened fields to the ANC-supporting settlement of Boipatong and massacred 46 people in scenes of unbelievable savagery. For example, a baby had part of his scalp axed off as his mother held him protectively in her arms. Residents claimed at the time, and in testimony to the Goldstone Commission, that police had protected the *impi*. Nelson Mandela declared the police were not fit to be called human, and angrily called off talks with government. 'I can no longer explain to our people why we continue to talk to a government who is murdering our people,' he said. De Klerk went to the area, but was forced to flee by furious township residents who beat on his car shouting, 'Go away you dog.' As his car sped off, police opened fire, killing three more residents.

The Goldstone Commission investigations into violence, which were headed by Judge Richard Goldstone, reported in 1993: 'No-one other than the Inkatha Freedom Party and the African National Congress have [sic] the power to curb the violence and intimidation being perpetrated by their respective supporters... . Even if allegations against members of the security forces prove to be justified, such misconduct would not have been possible but for the ongoing battle between the ANC and the IFP.' The commission criticized ANC and Inkatha leadership for being 'overhasty' in levelling accusations at each other, and for being 'tardy' in taking steps to 'stop the violence by imposing discipline and accountability among membership'.

Prolonged political violence, of the type that occurred in South Africa, sees an almost total collapse in conventional policing. The police became paramilitary in nature and, assisted by security legislation which permitted detention and obliquely condoned torture, police failed to investigate crime.

Criminal statistics became submerged as part of 'the violence'. Ordinary communities began arming themselves and adopting vigilantism to protect themselves, not only against political opponents, but also the gangs of criminals that roamed free under the mantle of 'the violence'. Some youth who attained political leadership but, because of years of lost schooling, could never obtain jobs, resorted to terror under the guise of political fiefdom.

Hostility between supporters of the Inkatha Freedom Party and the African National Congress continued to cause violence in KwaZulu-Natal after the 1994 general election.

*Before the Inkatha Freedom
Party agreed to participate in
the 1994 general election,
violence kept flaring up in the
East Rand, here at Thokoza.*

Courts failed to operate properly, as all of society took on the propaganda that all violence was politically motivated. Criminal activity, thus obscured, thrived.

The faction fighting, a centuries-old scourge, was allowed to flourish and develop new forms under the smoke haze of violence. Ultimately society itself was in danger for, after the political causes disappear and communities remain heavily armed, fearful and vengeful, what or whom do they then have to blame?

Violence took other forms. In a series of train massacres, people were shot in their seats as they travelled to work or were thrown out of trains. In one instance an entire carriage of devout Christians, who held church services as they travelled to and from work, were executed as they prayed and sang hymns. Truth and Reconciliation Commission hearings later heard confessions from the government agents who carried out these atrocities.

The ANC's document on counter revolution had correctly surmised that, '... the character of the violence engulfing the PWV [now Gauteng] in particular ... is organized counter revolution carried out by well-trained, professional bandits. The actions are thoroughly planned and while the immediate actors might not have any political programme the controllers are pursuing definite political objectives.

'The actions are characterized by deliberate terrorism. The actions of these units is not an aberration, but reflects the confidence of forces acting within the ambit of state policy with the support of command structures all the way up – the state is creating an excuse for repressive measures – switching violence on/off at given moments to create the impression that the state is indispensable to the achievement of peace in the townships... .'

Buthelezi, who became Home Affairs Minister in Mandela's government, wears the wounds which ANC insults have inflicted upon him like medals. Sitting in his office at parliament in 1998, he said: 'These things are still there, they are not behind us. You can't leave things like that without passing through a period of reconciliation. People cannot say the IFP and ANC can merge. We need to quietly sit and clear this up.'

Buthelezi says Mandela was his hero, with the emphasis on *was*. Insiders say Mandela has often come close to bullying in negotiations with Buthelezi, '... which just makes Mangosuthu stubborn'. But, Buthelezi clearly respects Mandela's successor, Thabo Mbeki: 'He shows more patience than the President. I don't think that once he has a point of view he cannot be converted.'

As the date set for the election approached, relations worsened between the ANC and Inkatha. Buthelezi began threatening that KwaZulu-Natal would ignore any negotiated settlement (Inkatha had already walked out of talks) and would go it alone. He called for an international negotiated settlement, to which Mandela finally agreed. Ultimately, though, this was a futile publicity ploy.

Elections happened relatively peacefully in KwaZulu-Natal, despite all the posturing of politicians and hundreds of funerals beforehand. Inkatha settled into an amicable relationship in the Government of National Unity, with Buthelezi proudly remarking in June 1998, 'So far I have served as acting president nine times when Mandela and Mbeki have been out of the country. It is a world record, and I am not even an ANC member.' On 27 August 1998, just over a month after Mandela turned 80, heading an organization with a host of strong leaders to take over from him on his retirement in 1999, Buthelezi celebrated his 70th birthday. Did Buthelezi have any intention of retiring? 'No, the work is hard, but it is there to be done.' Was he grooming any successors – none were apparent? 'Having been born an *nkosi* [chief], I would like to enjoy the last years of my life, but I have been born into a tradition of service. I think I have served as best I can. If there were younger leaders who could take over, maybe. But I have always said that when we attained political liberation, that is when the liberation struggle will really begin, and that is only starting now.'

Mandela doesn't walk on water, he roller blades. He has a core of autocratic, ruthless steel.

Senior Inkatha Freedom
Party parliamentarian

Transformation

Does it firmly put us on the
road to majority rule and
how long will it take?

Nelson Mandela
Discussing a proposed agreement from
the Multiparty Talks, 1993

Pages 118 and 119: Nelson Mandela and his two deputy presidents Thabo Mbeki and FW de Klerk.

Below: Mandela welcomes his old friend Oliver Tambo back from exile, December 1990.

Mac Maharaj recalls, 'Late one night in 1993, when we thought that we had finally made a breakthrough after marathon talks, the ANC's negotiation team went to report to Madiba at his Johannesburg home.' Even though a legal man with a fine eye and an appreciation of detail, the president of the ANC had only two questions for his exhausted negotiators: Does it put us firmly on the road to majority rule and how long will it take?

'Satisfied with our answers on both, he gave the interim constitution his blessing. That grasp of unshakeable principle and purpose is a measure of the man Nelson Mandela – the legend known around the world as Madiba. ... Perhaps the greatness of Nelson Mandela was at no time more evident that in his management of the negotiations that led to democratic rule, or even in the years that followed the finest, most benevolent, most caring presidency South Africa had experienced in more than three centuries of Western type rule.' Democratic negotiations took place in a huge warehouse close to Johannesburg International Airport. It was the perfect negotiations venue, with dozens of small offices and rooms for political parties, journalists and other organizations to caucus, have offices and hold discussions. The large central hall was big enough to hold the 28 political organizations involved in the multiparty talks, and versatile enough to be sectioned off into smaller sections. Talks frequently went on until 2 or 3 a.m. and resumed a few hours later. The workers in the canteen adjacent to the hall kept delegates supplied with steaming mugs of coffee at all hours of the day, and provided plates of porridge for breakfast and stews for meals later in the day or in the early hours of the morning.

The [apartheid] government was a set of committees that shuffled papers between each other, rigid, bureaucratic, and unresponsive to the needs of society, even white society.

Jay Naidoo (Minister of Posts, Telecommunications and Broadcasting), 1998

Right from the start right-wing Afrikaners, joined by foreign hangers-on and some English members, were radically opposed to the unbanning of organizations and the release of political prisoners, indeed any action that recognized the human rights of black people and that could pave the way to their assuming government in South Africa.

Between April and mid-July 1990, two people were killed and 48 others injured around Johannesburg in a dozen right-wing bombings directed at places such as taxi-ranks where black people congregated. Arms were being stolen from police stations, armouries and defence force caches. Some people said the leader of the right-wing Afrikaner Weerstandsbeweging Eugene Terre'Blanche was an agent for military intelligence and that the bombs were a ploy to destabilize or prevent democratic elections. By the time the Truth and Reconciliation Commission hearings had ended in 1998 this accusation did not seem far-fetched.

David Ottaway, in his book *Chained Together*, wrote that the personal relationship between Mandela and De Klerk '... fell victim to the violence. They became increasingly disillusioned with each other, questioning the ability of the other to deliver his constituency and discovering they held strikingly different views of how the new South Africa should be governed. Each accused the other of "talking peace while making war". The peace process was made more difficult by the failure of both leaders to respect either the letter or the spirit of the first series of preliminary accords they reached. ... They spent as much time negotiating with their allies as they did with each other. Small wonder then, that not a single accord struck between May 1990 and September 1992, whether over the release of political prisoners, the return of exiles, the ANC's hidden arms cache, or the curbing of violence, was carried out on time or according to the letter.

'Mandela launched vicious personal verbal attacks against De Klerk that left one wondering why he was still talking to the state president at all. He also sometimes lacked political courage, shrinking from chastizing his own followers for the same excesses in violence he accused ANC opponents of indulging in. ... De Klerk who had the power of the state and its security apparatus to make things happen if he willed, failed to act. It took a third party, Judge Richard Goldstone [who headed a commission investigating state security's role in the political violence], to point out that both Mandela and De Klerk were partly responsible for the political violence, and that both had duties to uphold as the country's two leading statesmen.'

As early as the ANC 8 January 1991 statement, 'Year of Mass Action for Transfer of Power to the People', Nelson Mandela gave the National Executive Committee (NEC) view that 'the government will have to take full responsibility for any delay to the constitutional negotiations caused by its failure to implement the agreements entered into at Groote Schuur and Pretoria. We will continue to use all means at our disposal to ensure that these agreements are adhered to, because of their intrinsic importance and their relevance to the process of an early state to the process of negotiating a new constitution.'

The ANC wanted the election of a constituent assembly to run the negotiations process and the establishment of 'an interim government to oversee the process of transition until a

Strain showing between Mandela and De Klerk at the signing of the National Peace Accord in 1991.

new parliament was elected and a democratic government formed on the basis of the new constitution'. While calling for the police and defence force to end conflict and the South African government to resign, the ANC also 'reaffirmed the right of the people to self-defence. By decision of our Consultative Conference, our movement is committed to assist the people throughout the country to set up the necessary mechanisms for the defence of each community, which mechanisms must enjoy the support and confidence of the people as a whole'. Mandela read this statement out slowly and ponderously in a small office used as the ANC boardroom in Munich Re, Johannesburg. Oliver Tambo sat stiffly beside him. This was one of his first public appearances back at home since his illness. His son Dali, who has become a well-known television personality in post-apartheid South Africa, stood at his side, elegant in a black Nehru suit. Journalists sat on the floor, squashed into every available space and spilling out into the passage.

The statement declared, 'We reaffirm our unwavering opposition to any of our members and supporters using force where political discussion is called for, or as a means of promoting any of our campaigns.' The two voices of the ANC were developing a public profile. It also said it would liaise with all relevant organizations to 'preclude violent confrontation ... we trust that all these organizations including IFP [Buthelezi's Inkatha Freedom Party] will cooperate with us in genuine good faith to save the lives and property of the people'.

On 29 January 1991, Mandela and Mangosuthu Buthelezi discussed ways to find peace in KwaZulu-Natal, but the accord they reached never had meaning among warring factions in the valleys and townships of KwaZulu-Natal or the areas around Johannesburg. Mandela was on a shortening fuse as violence escalated, with dozens of people dying almost daily.

Mandela addressed a closed-door meeting of US Congress members and their aides in Cape Town on 3 April, during which he delivered a tirade against FW de Klerk for the continuing violence. The following day he finally bowed to criticism from his rank and file and told the ANC National Executive Committee meeting that he had been wrong to call De Klerk a 'man of integrity.' The next day, the ANC delivered an ultimatum, which it publicized, giving De Klerk until 9 May to take seven steps to end violence or talks would cease. Talks were on a knife edge.

The process again approached collapse when, on 19 July, newspapers published details showing the government had helped fund Inkatha, including giving it money for rallies held in November 1988 and March 1989. The newspapers also said they had evidence that government was supplying Inkatha with guns and giving military training to its cadres.

Foreign Minister Pik Botha held a press conference, which was carefully edited before being broadcast, at South African Broadcasting Corporation television studios. During this conference journalists accused the government of duplicity and being involved in the murders of hundreds of civilians in KwaZulu-Natal. A sanguine Botha denied all the published facts (which the TRC has subsequently shown were true) and dismissed the accusations of journalists as hysterical propaganda.

On 14 September, a national peace conference was held in Johannesburg under pressure from church groups and civil society. This was the first face-to-face meeting of Mandela, De Klerk and Buthelezi on one platform. Their unhappy faces in photographs reflect the mood, portending the failure of the meeting. A Peace Accord was drawn up and signed by all parties but it might as well have been in invisible ink for the commitment those signatures carried. Civil society had, however, made its will known: it wanted talks to continue.

OPPOSITE: Nelson Mandela in a relaxed mood during the March 1992 referendum.

From 28 to 29 November, 60 delegates from 20 parties held talks at a hotel near Johannesburg International Airport to lay the ground rules for multiparty talks. The Pan-Africanist Congress (PAC) walked out on the second day.

It seemed as if the Christmas season might bring goodwill, with the Convention for a Democratic South Africa (Codesa) beginning on 20 December with 18 delegations and government. Buthelezi refused to attend but sent delegates. Goodwill was a faint hope that rapidly dissipated. De Klerk spoke at the end of the first session, saying government was not against an interim multiracial government and that a power-sharing model could be made.

*I was wrong to call
FW de Klerk a
man of integrity.*

NELSON MANDELA
TO THE ANC NATIONAL EXECUTIVE
COMMITTEE MEETING, 4 APRIL 1991

He went on to question the ANC's right to participate in the convention by saying the ANC had not declared the whereabouts of its secret arms cache and was maintaining a private army. A visibly angry Mandela strode to the podium as De Klerk stepped off it. Mandela said the Nationalists were pursuing a double agenda by talking peace, while 'conducting a war'. He added that De Klerk was 'not fit to be president'. Matters did not improve. The initial Codesa talks were relatively brief, and were succeeded by bilateral talks.

After a major defeat in a by-election in Potchefstroom for the National Party, De Klerk called a referendum on his policies on 17 March. There was a huge turnout at the polls, and 68.6 percent of the all-white voters showed their support of negotiations.

*RIGHT: The national peace
conference of 14 September 1991
was the first face-to-face
appearance of Nelson Mandela,
FW de Klerk and Mangosuthu
Buthelezi on one platform.
A peace accord was signed but it
failed to have any real effect.*

On 17 June 1992, an Inkatha *impi* from the KwaMadala hostel at Iscor's steel works south of Johannesburg massacred 46 people at the primarily ANC settlement of Boipatong including an eight-month-old baby who was held in his mother's arms. Three days later De Klerk visited Boipatong but was not able to leave his car (*see also* page 114). The ANC suspended all political contacts with the government.

On 16 November, Judge Goldstone announced that his commission had conducted an unprecendented raid on Military Intelligence's covert operations centre and had uncovered files of data

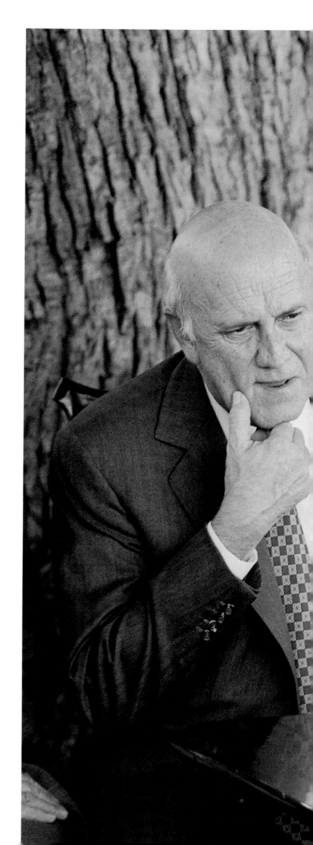

about state involvement in assassinations and covert fomenting of violence. De Klerk appointed the Steyn Commission which, a month later, suspended or retired 23 officers, in what was seen as a facile damage control exercise.

On 12 February 1993 the ANC and government announced an agreement in principle on a five-year transition. During this transition, a government of national unity, formed by the main election winners, would govern. On 5 March Codesa talks were finally resumed. Delegates burned the midnight oil as they raced toward a 1994 election date. They were still leaping countless hurdles, particularly those imposed by right-wing violence, which

included bombings and killings. Codesa held its third plenary session on 1 April, with 25 parties, including the white right-wing Conservative Party, participating. Right-wing thugs drove an armoured vehicle into the multiparty talks centre, making an aggressive, but ultimately futile, threat.

What had a more profound effect, however, was the assassination on 10 April of the most popular man in the ANC, the SACP Secretary General and former Umkhonto we Sizwe leader. Chris Hani, a man who had gone out of his way to reconcile, was murdered in the driveway of his home by a right-wing Polish immigrant Janus Walusz, in conspiracy with Conservative Party leader, Clive Derby-Lewis. The death threw the country into grief. The turmoil the right-wing hoped would result never happened, as ANC leaders appealed for calm and disciplined behaviour.

More sadness was in store for the ANC. Fourteen days later, Oliver Tambo, president of the ANC from 1967 to 1991 (when Mandela was elected), died of a stroke at the age of 75 with his family at his side. If anything, these two blows firmed Mandela's resolve and that of the ANC: there was no time to waste.

In the final days of apartheid South Africa seemed to sink into mayhem. The Freedom Alliance was formed between Inkatha and right-wing Afrikaners, war talk abounded, and Afrikaners threatened to secede from South Africa. Sixty-nine towns, in what was then the Transvaal and 50 elsewhere, extending in a sickle down the centre of the country, called themselves *Volkstaats* (people's states). Standerton (in present-day Mpumalanga), a town of 15,000 whites and 65,000 blacks that was ruled by white councillors, called itself a

LEFT: A rare sign of friendship between Nelson Mandela and FW de Klerk during the Codesa talks.

Volkstaat in November 1993. It was immediately crippled by a black consumer boycott of the town's businesses. Whites walked around with side-arms strapped to their waists in holsters and black people joined the militant anti-white PAC. When white businesspeople realized the boycott was destroying them financially, they began pressurizing for change. One Standerton businessman complained that he had lost the contract for an eleven-million rand factory to be put up by foreign investors when they realized Standerton had called itself a *Volkstaat*. Bophuthatswana (a 'homeland') threatened to declare unilateral independence, as did KwaZulu-Natal under Buthelezi.

There seemed no end to barbarity. Mandela's soft demeanour with a ready smile became sad, even though freedom seemed so close.

OPPOSITE: Nelson Mandela, carrier of hopes, implementer of dreams.

BELOW: Nelson Mandela is surrounded by a throng of people in an election campaign visit to Khayelitsha, Cape Town, in September 1993.

The 1994 election process, which was the first democratic election held in South Africa, was beset with numerous flaws. There was chaos in many areas of the country on the ballot days, as violent elements attempted to sway voters, or intimidate them into staying away from the polls.

The first day of elections, for pregnant women and for the elderly, was 26 April 1994. In the rural regions of KwaZulu-Natal elderly people, when asked where they had come from, would look towards the blue hills on the distant horizon and say they had walked for two, or even, three days. Most were barefoot, some had a single shoe. They sat in the hot sun, without water, food or ablution facilities, patiently waiting to cast their first vote, which had been denied them fifty years or even longer. Some slept in the open air under the cold night skies waiting for the polling booths to open the following day. Nothing was more precious than this first, centuries-elusive vote.

After several long days, during which the ballot papers were counted, Nelson Rolihlahla Mandela, who had himself voted for the first time ever at the age of 75, was elected as the president of South Africa.

*A serious Nelson Mandela
going over his speech prior
to his inauguration as South
Africa's first democratically
elected president.*

*As invariably happens
when the time comes to
gather the harvest, many
have appeared in our midst
who claim that they, and
not the millions who
sustained the struggle for
many decades under the
leadership of the ANC,
are the ones who planted
the seed and tended the
tree of freedom.*

NELSON MANDELA

8 JANUARY 1996 STATEMENT

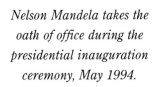

Nelson Mandela takes the oath of office during the presidential inauguration ceremony, May 1994.

On 10 May 1994, Nelson Mandela was inaugurated as State President with Thabo Mbeki and Frederick de Klerk as his deputy presidents. Six thousand delegates from around the world attended the ceremony, including Britain's Duke of Edinburgh and Palestine's Yasser Arafat. For South Africans the time of deepest emotion came not when Nelson Mandela made his pledges as president, but when the airforce flew by in salute. Six helicopters bore the new flag; the defence force had bowed to democracy.

In the presence of those assembled here, and in the full realization of the high calling I assume as executive President in the service of the Republic of South Africa, I, Nelson Rolihlahla Mandela, do hereby swear to be faithful to the Republic of South Africa, and do solemnly and sincerely promise at all times to promote that which will advance, and oppose all that may harm the Republic, to obey, observe, uphold and maintain the Constitution and all other laws of the Republic, to discharge my duties with all my strength and talents to the best of my knowledge and ability and, true to the dictates of my conscience, to do justice to the well-being of the Republic and all its people. So help me God.

Within three months violence was a distant memory. Government had laid out the plans of an ambitious vision, the Reconstruction and Development Programme. It had announced a Truth and Reconciliation Commission with far-reaching amnesty clauses. More black families moved into wealthy, previously white neighbourhoods. Black entrepreneurs set up stands on the sidewalks of suburbs where they would never before have dreamed of establishing a business. Hope had finally come home to South Africa.

At the end goodwill prevailed

At the end the bloodletting stopped.
At the end, goodwill prevailed.
At the end the overwhelming
majority, both black and white,
decided to invest in peace.

President Nelson Mandela
To the Joint Houses of the Congress
of the United States of America,
6 October 1994

PAGES 138 AND 139:
Nelson Mandela at his presidential residence.

The premier newspaper of Kampala, Uganda, *The Monitor*, wrote in a tribute to President Mandela, the day before his eightieth birthday in 1998: 'There is no known accolade which has not been bestowed upon Mandela. International media often refer to him as the only living saint – at least the only saint who is also a politician. In Africa, in particular, Mandela inevitably looms larger than life. This is a continent where politicians never tell the truth, nor leave power gracefully even when their rule is hated by nearly all the people, and their countries have turned into a wreck.

'Mandela said he would serve one term, and he is living up to his word. Last year, he chose to hand over the leadership of the ruling ANC to his heir-apparent Thabo Mbeki. Next year he is set to leave the presidency. He has already relinquished most of the functions of the office. In South Africa itself, Mandela's rule has brought its share of disappointments. Crime is still rampant. Promises of economic empowerment and housing for millions of black South Africans who were victims of apartheid have not been met, and the people are angry and feeling let down. But dismantling the legacy of apartheid, and making all the blacks rich could not have been Mandela's main job. Mandela showed that it was possible to rise beyond the politics of hate, race, and that any price is worth paying for a democracy. That it is possible to live in harmony with one's jailer.'

When southern Africa went to war in August 1998 – Zimbabwe, Angola and Namibia on the side of Democratic Republic of Congo President Laurent Kabila, and Uganda and Rwanda to attack him – Nelson Mandela, as chairman of the Southern African Development Community, spent entire weekends and long nights trying to bring about peace. After the first weekend it looked as though he had brokered a ceasefire, but war again broke out, one of many conflicts that stymied the hopes for peace and growth in Africa. The position echoed that at the turn of the nineteenth century when Congo was fighting Belgian colonialists. Congo's battle to be free of undemocratic rule would last for the rest of the twentieth century.

In 1882, thirty years before the founding of the Native National Congress (later the ANC), one of its fathers, the Reverend John L Dube, wrote, 'Oh! How I long for that day when darkness and gloom shall have passed away because the Sun of Righteousness has risen with healing in his hand. This shall be the dawning of a brighter day for the people of Africa.'

In 1906, Pixley kaIsaka Seme wrote of the 'regeneration of Africa' and an end to 'the demon of racialism, the aberrations of the Xhosa-Fingo feud, the animosity that exists between the Zulus and the Tongas, between the Basutos and every other native must be buried and forgotten: it has shed among us sufficient blood. We are one people. These divisions, these jealousies, are the cause of all our woes and of all our backwardness and ignorance today'.

What had changed in 100 years of African history? A man who saw peace as the ultimate goal arose from the belly of persecution. He recognized that reconciliation meant extending a hand first to one's enemies: trying to understand and allay their fears and bring them into the circle of one's friends, making them understand that for their own peace of mind and progress the most difficult task had to be accomplished first – negotiating peace with their foes. And giving them reason to feel safe in territory that they, too, had before considered hostile.

Sheila Camerer, a leading member of parliament in the National Party, said of Mandela, 'He is the only president I have known around parliament who never rushes by ordinary MP's smiling and waving. He always stops and takes trouble to greet you personally. It must be hell for the minders who are trying to get him to the next meeting.' She recalls an early evening function when she was sworn in as Deputy Minister in Mandela's government of National Unity: '... my mother who has difficulty walking, also attended. After the ceremony everyone moved through to the next room where cocktails and snacks were served and a string quartet was playing. My mother, who had been sitting in a corner somehow got left out of the general move, which he [Mandela] spotted. He went across and gave her his arm and escorted her through to the party, which of course has left her an undying admirer.'

Nelson Mandela adores women and they him. Here, on one of his informal neighbourhood walk-abouts he is greeted by residents of a housing complex.

At the end goodwill prevailed

141

It was not only his South African people he charmed. Terror Lekota, ANC chairman from December 1997, reflected: 'Mandela won over the international community to give maximum support to this fledgling democracy. From the point of view of superpowers, we needed the friendship of countries like the USA and Britain, but not at any cost. Nelson has created a place for South Africa as a model of conflict resolution and has begun to cut us out as international advocates of peace. His intervention in the Democratic Republic of Congo, in Indonesia, and then Ireland and the Angolan conflict were examples of his role as peacemaker, and a recognition of South Africans, with their negotiating skills as peace brokers.

'Although we had an alliance with the South African Communist Party we were not against a market economy, we became committed to it. Mandela went to South Africa's business community and made a huge impact on them, swinging them around to be supportive of this government in a manner very few could have done.'

Mandela led by example, speaking again and again of the 'great importance to assert the primacy of social morality among our people'. He said this morality needed to 'form part of a new patriotism which should inspire and motivate the majority of our people'. It needed to combat lawlessness, corruption, terror, and disregard for the norms of a just and equitable society: '... we must continue the struggle to give life to what we said in the Freedom Charter – that South Africa belongs to all who live in it, black and white, and that no government can justly claim authority unless it is based on the will of the people as a whole. But the national reconciliation for which we continue to struggle cannot be founded on the preservation and perpetuation of the old order of white privilege and black deprivation. True reconciliation does not consist in merely forgetting the past. It does not rest with black forgiveness,

The Princess of Wales visited South Africa shortly before her death in 1997. As well as sharing a great love for children, she and President Mandela had a remarkable rapport.

sensitivity to white fears and tolerance of an unjust status quo on one hand, and white gratitude and appreciation underlined by a tenacious clinging to exclusive privilege on the other. It has to be based on the creation of a truly democratic, nonracial and non-sexist society. A serious challenge faces our white compatriots to grasp fully the importance of their role in the efforts to achieve national reconciliation. ... Vengeance is not our goal. The building of a new nation at peace with itself because it is reconciled with its past is our objective.'

Speaking to the ANC's national conference in December 1997 Mandela said: 'We seek not just freedom but opportunity – not just legal equity but human ability – not just equality as a right and a theory, but equality as a fact and as a result. We have experienced serious resistance to the transformation of the public service, with representatives of the old order using all means in their power to ensure that they remain in dominant positions.'

Reflecting deeper on the sort of president and leader Mandela would become, Maharaj said, 'Both before and after April 1994 we felt his deep sense of genuine empathy and concern about the people of this country, including white people, for which he was criticized for reaching out the hand of reconciliation too far. Children have a keener sense of his genuine humility and warmth. Wherever he goes they swamp him while their parents are more intimidated by the imposing stature of a great man. He rejoices in the joy of others. This is the secret behind his sunshine smile. It's part of his hands-on approach to everything. It's the intuitive feel that doesn't require image consultants and publicity agents'. Mandela made a point of going to children who were in trauma, whether a child dying of cancer, or another shot in a vicious attack. He regularly visited the schools of his grandchildren where he would sit on the floor with the children and listen to their comments and stories.

He said that he missed children more than anything else while in prison, particularly on Robben Island. His sheer pleasure in their company and their instinctive trust of him said more than a thousand words. Not for Mandela the politician's kiss of a baby – he would push adults aside to give a child an opportunity to speak or hold his hand. His Children's Fund became the wealthiest welfare organization in the country. He would take businesspeople to his birthplace in Qunu and ask for their help in rehabilitating the schools in the area.

Mandela was the president of reconciliation and peace, the foundation which South Africa most needed. Maharaj recalls, 'We all remember his hand reaching out to FW de Klerk at the end of a tense harsh live TV debate in the run-up to the 1994 elections; his donning of the Springbok rugby No. 6 jersey at the World Cup Final; his appearances in communities gripped by fear generated by violence as in Richmond and the Cape Flats; his visit to Betsie Verwoerd [the widow of apartheid's architect Hendrik Verwoerd] in Orania; his systematic and continuous reaching out to Mangosuthu Buthelezi; the phone call or the unexpected visit... .

'Many who accompany him on his punishing schedule criss-crossing the length and breadth of South Africa on visits to communities come out exhausted, but he emerges energized and revitalized'. His 1994 election campaign schedule was so gruelling that the media assigned rotating teams after their young reporters complained of exhaustion.

As the ANC began governing, it found divisions widening between itself and its followers. Maharaj reflects 'The historic responsibilities placed on the ANC have multiplied. Maintaining and continuously re-energizing the ANC as the political instrument for mobilization and transformation must now go side by side with the task of ensuring that the ANC in government ... draws together the entire nation-in-making into effecting transformation. By exhortation and his actions Madiba asks that we continuously deepen our links with the people'.

Terror Lekota agrees: 'Before we came to government we had only our organization to service, now we have government too. We took a lot of our most experienced people and put them in government. We should have left some to continue running the organization'.

The ANC may have battled to retain cohesion, but the gains made for ordinary South Africans were multitudinous. Mandela said in his address to the joint houses of the congress of the USA on 6 October 1994: 'The time that has passed has allowed me to come back to you to speak not of a dream deferred, of which your fellow countryman Langston Hughes spoke. The history that cannot be unmade has enabled me to repeat in this Chamber the power of the triumph of the oppressed. For, as the representatives of centuries of white minority rule bowed to the results of the democratic process, the people did, as your fellow countryman, Martin Luther King Jr did, cry out: "Free at last, free at last, thank God Almighty we are free at last!" Both black and white in our country can say today we are brother and sister to one another, a united rainbow nation that derives its strength from the bonding of its many races and colours, constitutes a celebration of the oneness of the human race...'.

In his last speech at the opening of parliament in February 1998 in Cape Town, Mandela reflected on the gains that had been made for ordinary people over the last three years, and how people could be mobilized 'to be their own liberators'. He pointed to some successes: 'Last year, we increased the supply of clean and accessible water from 700,000 to 1.3 million South Africans. We surpassed our plans to build or upgrade 500 clinics last year. The primary school feeding scheme reaches 4.9 million children. We will make 421,000 telephone connections this year. In 1997 we made 400,000 electricity connections, meaning South Africa has reached a 58 percent electrification level. The law on secure land tenure will bring more certainty into the lives of over six million citizens. We are at the beginning of an arduous and protracted struggle for a better quality of life. In the course of this struggle, we shall have immediate successes; we shall have setbacks; but we shall progress, inch by inch, towards our goal. Measures to eliminate corruption have uncovered many fraudsters in the government machinery. Some public servants are, to put it mildly, not imbued with the spirit of public service. Even in instances where funds are available, they do not turn up on time or they relate to senior citizens with attitudes bordering on the criminal.'

One of Mandela's key cabinet ministers, Jay Naidoo, said, 'We had to work within the constraints of a government designed to deal with the needs of a small minority. Transformation in terms of policies, laws and institutions, budgets, civil service and delivery mechanisms, all constitutes governance. How do you deliver in an innovative and creative way and transform orthodoxy to revolutionary? We had to transform the way we deliver services – citizens

True reconciliation does not consist in merely forgetting the past. It does not rest with black forgiveness, sensitivity to white fears and tolerance of an unjust status quo on one hand, and white gratitude and appreciation underlined by a tenacious clinging to exclusive privilege on the other. It has to be based on the creation of a truly democratic, nonracial and nonsexist society.

NELSON MANDELA
ANC CONFERENCE, 1997

Nelson Mandela with his grandson Bambatha.

At the end goodwill prevailed

are the main customers of government – we had to change the culture and value system. You must not underestimate transition. It was bold, courageous and risky. Obviously the charisma of Mandela has been important but what underpinned that were a set of circumstances that were a compromise. We did not win a military victory, it was a compromise. The Sunset Clause [which guaranteed civil servants their jobs for a time] created a sense of security for this. Difficulties around the transformation of the civil service had more to do with our own weaknesses than the Sunset Clause. We fundamentally restructured this department [Posts and Telecommunications] down from 400 to 200. We reshaped policies, strategies and delivery systems. We are still trying to revitalize the civil service and transform its leadership. We have to get the culture right so that civil servants know they are there to deliver to the people. We have too much on paper and not enough in practice. The question is not vision, it is strategy. Mandela has been an anchor for stabilizing the transition, his status, charisma, his warmth, his humility and the sacrifice that he made without being embittered was a very important anchor not just for us, but especially for whites and Afrikaners. He had visionary leadership that emphasized reconciliation. When we were being criticized by militants in our own ranks that we were overdoing reconciliation, he said: "What does it cost for us to reconcile? What is taking money from our government to meet the needs of the white minority? The most significant slice of budgetary resources is toward closing the development gap with health, education and telephones". And people had no answer to that. His leadership has been important, even though he has not been correct all the time.

'One of the most exciting periods of our history has been the last 50 years of struggle and the most exciting period the first five years of government. It inspired people and made them part of rebuilding.'

OPPOSITE: President Nelson Mandela with a victorious Bafana Bafana captain Neil Tovey at the African Nations Cup soccer tournament in 1995.

TOP LEFT: President Mandela proudly donned a Springbok Number 6 jersey when he awarded the World Cup trophy to rugby captain François Pienaar in 1995.

ABOVE: Dressed in a South African cricket blazer and cap, the President congratulates big-hitting Adrian Kuiper after the South Africa/New Zealand match at Port Elizabeth on 22 January 1996.

At the end goodwill prevailed

The nation's darling: Nelson
Mandela is enthusiastically
embraced by a nurse at a
Gauteng hospital.

Many cabinet ministers, exhausted after long years spent in hiding from the police and separated for months or years from their families while in jail or in hiding, had hoped democracy would give them time with their families. It was a wan hope. Naidoo, a devoted husband and father, noted: 'Frank Chikane [a senior Mbeki aide] said being in government is very antisocial, very anti-family. I have so little time with my kids and that's having a devastating impact on them.

'Mbeki will have easier choices, there is more talent to choose from, he will be unfettered by patronage. Mandela had to balance exiles, trade unions, the United Democratic Front and the old government.'

Terror Lekota says, 'Mandela had a vision of a united country which he developed with his policy of national reconciliation. He piloted that more than anyone among our ranks. He also considered it very important for stability that the supporters of minority parties should be protected. Nelson was able to assure the international community of our commitment to democracy. He won them over to give maximum support to this fledgling democracy.'

Mandela extended consideration and thoughtfulness even to members of opposition parties. In 1998, the so-called Meiring Report alleged a coup plot against government, which even a cursory reading of the report indicated was ridiculous – alleged coup plotters including conspirators as unlikely as Winnie Madikizela-Mandela and pop star Michael Jackson. Political parties were allowed to see the report but made to sign secrecy oaths.

Sheila Camerer was instructed by her party, the National Party, to read the report on behalf of her leader Marthinus van Schalkwyk, who was overseas. She recalls, 'When ... the Democratic Party started alleging in the Press that I was spilling the beans although I'd signed the secrecy undertaking, he [Mandela] rang me up and assured me he was quite happy with all my statements. This was before he said so to the media.' President Mandela, and not her own party, sprang to her defence first. This was not the first or the only occasion that he did this for fellow members of parliament – regardless of their political party.

But, after uniting his people, Mandela gave all his followers and party leaders the challenge that troubled him most, the task without which democracy would be imperilled: to end poverty and create a society based on economic justice for all. In his speech to the joint houses of the US Congress in 1994, Mandela underpinned his greatest desire, and the challenge of the millennium to come, when he said: 'As we look and look again at the reality that freedom brings, we see together with TS Eliot that we are, still:

> In the uncertain hour before the morning
> Near the ending of interminable night
> At the recurrent end of the unending ...
> While the dead leaves still rattled on like tin
> Over the asphalt where no other sound was'.

The rattle of leaves was a symbol for the echo of poverty, the '... pervasive poverty that afflicts our society; the despair of millions who are without jobs and without hope, the unborn who we know will be born disabled and die before their maturity

because of poverty; the darkness that engulfs millions because they are illiterate and innumerate; the many who will be victims of rape, robbery and other violent crimes because hunger, want and brutalization have warped and condemned many a human soul... .

'The new age will surely demand that democracy must also mean a life of plenty. As the images of life lived anywhere on the globe become available to all, so will the contrast between rich and the poor within and across frontiers, and within and across continents, become a motivating force impelling the deprived to demand a better life from the powers that be, whatever their location.

'As the possibility of nations to become islands sufficient unto themselves diminishes and vanishes forever, so will it be that the suffering of the one shall, at the same time, inflict pain upon the other.' He said this may mean that technology will succeed in doing what all the great thinkers failed to do: prove that 'we are all part of one, indivisible and common humanity'.

At the end of more than three hundred years of colonialism, war and injustice God blessed South Africa with Nelson Rolihlahla Mandela. At the end God blessed Africa, giving a guide for her people to make them strong. For the life and leadership of Nelson Mandela ... just a man, but a most extraordinary man, who led and brought peace and showed us the meaning of moral justice – we as South Africans give thanks.

Nelson Mandela greets a group of women on National Women's Day.

A golden age

I have a dream, that one day all men will be free.

MARTIN LUTHER KING

Govan Mbeki, one of Nelson Mandela's oldest friends, ponders after being asked to give what he believes will be the differences in the presidential styles of Thabo Mbeki, and Mandela. 'The difference,' he finally says, 'is that Nelson is tall, and Thabo is short'. To follow in the shoes of Nelson Mandela is an impossible task, but Thabo Mbeki has already shown that he will not even try. Sensibly, he will forge his own path. For his part, Nelson Mandela has long been aware of widespread fears about 'what will happen after Mandela goes', and of the potentially damaging economic implications of such fears. Two and a half years into his five-year presidency, Nelson Mandela began shifting more and more of the responsibility for the day-to-day running of government to his deputy.

Both Mandela and Mbeki reason that, the fewer surprises the country experiences, the steadier its economic growth will remain. Mandela even delivered a controversial speech, drafted by his successor, to the ANC conference in December 1997. This address, which attacked the media, whites for failing to reform, and international donors for not upholding their promises, was torn apart by critics. The ANC attempted damage control, but the hectoring words could not be erased. Why did Mandela read a speech which he probably knew would be widely criticized? A senior African National Congress official said: 'Mandela was not happy with the speech, although he agreed with some of its content. But he also knew that if Mbeki delivered a speech like that it would cause him and the country grave damage, but because of Mandela's stature the speech could be carried off – still with the harshest criticism of Mandela's presidency, but without causing damage to the economy.'

Who is this man who will follow Mandela? A member of Mbeki's so-called kitchen cabinet, one of the groups of educationists, religious leaders, businesspeople and others that he meets with at least once a month, confesses to unease that Mbeki allows people to praise him in his presence, saying, 'It is very unAfrican'. That, an ANC cabinet member muses, is in part why South Africans battle to understand Mbeki: 'He is more British than African. His university education was in Britain. And, whereas Mandela shows African qualities such as affection toward ordinary people, and consultation, Thabo is more reserved, more British.'

The premier of a province puts the difference in leadership styles down to the experiences of the two men during the period that the ANC was banned. Mbeki left the country at the age of 19 and went into exile. His experience was of an ANC where Umkhonto we Sizwe was its hope and mantra, and where obedience to rules from the top was an essential part of survival. Mandela, however, lived for 27 years in prison where consultation and cooperation was essential to survival. Robben Island prisoners developed a complex, but highly effective, network of consultation, negotiation, discussion and decision-making. This recognized the equity of all, and an aversion to 'the cult of leadership', that is one person having overriding authority. That in turn influenced the United Democratic Front and the Congress of South African Trade Unions when both were formed in the mid-1980s. Many believe internal strife within the ANC today is caused by those two disciplines failing to understand the operational styles of the other – the former is profoundly consultative and democratic, while the latter operates more like top levels of business: consultation happens only among a limited coterie of leadership and those below are expected to obey. This is an important reason why ANC interference in leadership decisions in the provinces, most particularly the Northern Province, Free State and Gauteng, led to open rebellion by a membership more used to UDF leadership styles.

Mbeki is seen as a man not to trifle with. While Mandela has tolerated gravely underperforming ministers, because of old loyalties, Mbeki will be unlikely to. Indres Naidoo, long

APARTHEID KILLS BAN APARTHEID

term ANC activist and parliamentarian, says Mandela, in his retirement, will be 'the father of the nation. He will continue ... reconciling conflict within South Africa, Africa and internationally'.

History adds an interesting dimension to an analysis of Mbeki, 'the man', and Mandela, 'the saint'. Photographs of Mandela up to his early 40s, before his incarceration, show a face with the haughtiness of the man who raised him, King Jongintaba. In old age he has earned the face of his beloved mother, a face of great sweetness. But Nelson Mandela has not always been sweet. He says his father 'had a proud rebelliousness, a stubborn sense of fairness, that I recognize in myself'. This is the man who with other ANC Youth Leaguers would, in the early 1940s, violently break up South African Communist Party (SACP) meetings. He had a firmness, bordering on arrogance, during the early 1960s. ANC parliamentarian Ben Turok repudiates the use of the word arrogant, pointing out that that period was a time of intense political struggle. Mandela had just finished a four-year Treason Trial with 156 others, including Turok. Apartheid laws were coming thick and fast, so were detentions, and resistance. Turok says: 'Mandela was fiery, a radical, although not an ideologue. But he was never the sort of man you would cuff on the back and say, hi'.

Turok, who knew Mbeki in exile, said he was 'much more withdrawn, more self-contained. He does not make friends easily, and is perhaps deeper in a way'. He says Mandela 'is not an intervener, a meddler or a fixer'. While Turok does not say it, Mbeki's interventions, particularly in the resolution of disputes between black people, are legendary. While Mandela has been the president

of peace and reconciliation, the essential seedbed for democracy, Mbeki will nurture within it the roots of economic justice, to ensure long-term democracy. Criticism has been levelled at Mbeki that, while Mandela reconciled, Mbeki dwells too much on race, mourning a South Africa divided by gross income disparities – primarily based on racial differences. But even the World Bank in 1998 said South Africa was the most 'unequal society in the world' and that real growth was impossible unless wage gaps were closed. As far back as his 1962 statement from the dock (*see also* page 29), Mandela said: 'Our complaint is not that we are poor by comparison with people in other countries, but that we are poor by comparison with the white people in our own country.'

Mandela's views have not always been moderate. When he came out of prison he was a solid supporter of nationalization and opposed to privatization. He also suggested 14-year-olds be given the vote. He once aptly said: 'Judge me not how I have risen, but how many times I have fallen and stood up again.' In the end, history will probably record that Nelson Mandela was, along with Mahatma Gandhi, one of the two greatest leaders of this century – one of the great leaders of any century.

This is South Africa's golden age, where terror at the top has been replaced by honour. Now the country needs to be governed – fine ideals have to be replaced with real progress – just as Gandhi was replaced by Nehru, one of the finest statesmen of this century. Mbeki does not have to wear Mandela's shoes or define the goals; he merely has to chart the route.

Perhaps all that Thabo Mbeki needs is to refer to a 1952 African National Congress handbook: 'Golden Rules for a Good Congress Member: Lead – don't Order! Congress members must be close to the people and trusted by them. They must lead, not dictate to the people.'

OPPOSITE: Midway through his five-year presidency Mandela began transferring responsibility for the day-to-day running of government to Thabo Mbeki so that there would be few surprises in store when Mbeki took over after the 1999 elections.

TOP LEFT: Thabo Mbeki with his wife of many years Zanele.

ABOVE: Thabo Mbeki and Graça Machel with a disabled child.

Mandela's legacy to South Africa is a dream, one that is shared by all South Africans. In Rabindranath Tagore's *Gitanjali*, which Mandela quoted when he wrote to accept the Jawaharlal Nehru Award from India in August 1980, Tagore describes a place

where the mind is without fear and the head is held high,
where knowledge is free;
where the world has been broken into
fragments by narrow domestic walls;
where words came out from the depths of truth;
where tireless striving stretches its arms towards perfection
where the clear stream of reason has not lost
its way into the dreary desert sand of dead habit;
where the mind is led forward by these into
ever widening thought and action
into that haven of Freedom, My Father, let my country awake.

The profound changes of the past four and a half years make the distance traversed so short, but with this epoch making progress, South Africa is in a momentous process of change toward a secure future. The time is yet to come for farewell. Many of us by choice or circumstance will not return. However, there is no time to pause, the long walk is not yet over. The prize of a better life has yet to be won.

PRESIDENT NELSON MANDELA'S FINAL SPEECH TO THE OPENING OF PARLIAMENT, 1999

Nelson Mandela, carrier of hopes, implementer of dreams

PAGES 158 AND 159: *Nelson Mandela poses for a farewell picture on the steps of parliament, at its 1999 opening, with Baleka Kgositsile, Patrick Lekota the chairman of the ANC and head of the National Council of Provinces, Mandela's wife Graça Machel, speaker of the house Frene Ginwala, deputy president Thabo Mbeki, his wife Zanele Mbeki, and Naledi Pandor speaker in the National Council of Provinces.*

ABOVE: *A new South Africa. Nelson Mandela takes his leave of a parliament filled with people of many colours, wearing many forms of dress, both modern and ethnic. Parliamentary speaker Frene Ginwala leads Mandela into the House, followed by Patrick Lekota.*

RIGHT: *Xhosa women, attired in traditional garb, sing their praises to the outgoing president.*

ABOVE: Siyagoba! *The people have spoken! Thabo Mbeki and Nelson Mandela salute the people at Soweto, three days before the June 1999 election.*

LEFT: Thabo Mbeki, the man anointed by Oliver Tambo as the 'crown prince' of the African National Congress, prepares to assume the leadership role from Nelson Mandela.

THIS PAGE: The time has come! Victory is ours! Nelson Mandela leads the African National Congress to an unprecedented electoral victory in South African politics in 1999, before taking a new walk to the tranquillity of a private life at his home in Qunu, Transkei, a reconstruction of his last prison – Victor Verster in Paarl.

THIS PAGE: Nelson Mandela and his wife, Graça Machel, in the garden of his Qunu home in December 1998, surrounded by the wealth of lives well lived – a large and vibrant family.

PAGE 164: From every ending, a new beginning: 'I am proud to vote for Thabo Mbeki.' Nelson Mandela casts his vote on 2 June 1999.

Index

Photographic credits

AB=Adil Bradlow AH=Anton Hammerl BG/T=Benny Gool/Trace EM=Eric Miller GH=George Hallett GI=Gallo Images GS=Great Stock HF=Henner Frankenfeld iA=iAfrika JdP=Jean du Plessis JS=Jürgen Schadeberg LG/T=Louise Gubb/Trace MC=Mayibuye Centre PNA=PictureNet Africa PV=Paul Velasco RB= Rodger Bosch SPA=South Photo Agency TA=The Argus

Front cover: Sasa Kralj/Trace; **Back cover:** GH; **Spine:** MC (top), BG/T (middle & bottom); **Front and back flap:** LG/T. **Pages:** 1 BG/T; **2–3** LG/T; **4–5** MC (top), PNA/HF (bottom); **6** BG/T (left & centre), LG/T (right); **8** MC; **9** BG/T; **11** MC (left, top & bottom), BG/T (top right), BG/TA (bottom right); **15** GS/JS; **16–19** MC; **21** Cape Archives; **23** MC; **24** GS/JS; **25** MC; **26** MC (top, centre & bottom left), GS/JS (bottom right); **27–32** MC; **33** Die Burger; **35–7** MC; **38** AH; **40–1** MC; **42** SPA; **43–7** MC; **48** LG/T; **49** Unknown photographer; **50** PNA/HF; **51** You & Me Images/ Gille de Vlieg (top), PNA/courtesy Nicodemus Sono (bottom); **52** JdP; **53** MC; **54** LG/T; **55** and **56** The Star/Themba Hadebe; **58–61** BG/T; **62–5** MC; **66** LG/T; **67** Mark Skinner; **68** MC; **70–1** MC (top); **71** Mark Widdicombe (bottom); **72** MC; **73** BG/T; **74** LG/T; **75–7** GS/JS; **78** BG/T; **81–9** MC; **90** LG/T; **91** MC; **92** LG/T; **94–6** MC; **98–9**

Reuters/Trace Images; **100–101** MC; **103** Ken Oosterbroek/GI; **104** RB/GI; **106** PNA/AB; **109** South Photo Agency; **110** LG/T; **112** PNA/Greg Marinovich; **113** EM/iA; **114** PV/GI; **115** João Silva; **116** GI; **119** JdP; **120** LG/T; **121** RB (top & bottom); **123** LG/T; **125** BG/T; **126** LG/T; **128** and **129** LG/T; **130–1** GH; **132** Associated Press/Denis Farrell; **133** LG/T; **135** GH; **136–7** LG/T; **138** BG/T; **141–3** GH; **144** JdP; **145** LG/T; **146** GI; **147** Allsport/David Rogers (left), TA (right); **148–50** BG/T; **153** MC; **154** AH; **155** PNA/Shaun Harris (left), BG/T (right); **156–160** BG/T; **161** PNA/Shaun Harris (top & bottom); **162** AP Photo/Jean-Marc Bujou (top left), AP Photo (top right), AB/Trace Images (bottom); **163** BG/T (top & bottom); **164** Reuters/Trace Images. **Endpapers (left page clockwise from top left)** GH (presidential bedroom), BG/T (with Graça on Blue Train), JdP (with garland), LG/T (with Winnie), PNA/PV (inauguration), MC (Mandela at 19), LG/T (on Zindzi's wedding day), PNA/HF (with FW de Klerk, Cyril Ramaphosa and Roelf Meyer); **(right page clockwise from top left)** LG/T (smiling Mandela), MC (daughter Zindzi), LG/T (with grandson Bambatha), The Star/Themba Hadebe (with Graça during 80th birthday celebrations), TA (lead-up to 1994 elections), BG/T (with Mangosuthu Buthelezi), MC (young Mandela), LG/T (embracing relative pop singer Brenda Fassie), PNA/AB (with deputy Thabo Mbeki).

Bibliography

This book was put together as a result of interviews, discussions and readings over a number of years with numerous South African figures, amongst them President Nelson Mandela. My life has been enriched by knowing, and in some instances having been the friend of, many great South Africans. Some of their recollections filter through into my work, but overall the work is mine. I have been blessed with important friendships including those with Helen Joseph, Tokyo Sexwale and Dali Tambo. Their reflections over the years have brought wisdom and, I hope, sensitivity, into my life and work. There were also interviews and discussions with key African National Congress leaders, Inkatha Freedom Party officials and others, people who did not wish attribution, but their contributions nonetheless helped guide my thinking and writing. This tribute to one of the greatest men of the twentieth century does not profess to be complete; time will bestow its own honours and great researchers. However, it contains more original research than any book published previously on this great man.

RESEARCH ESTABLISHMENTS:
Where no reference is made to a research establishment, the book, document or interview forms part of my own personal collection.
- Mayibuye Centre, University of the Western Cape, Cape Town (MC)
- South African Library, Cape Town (SAL)
- Personal collection, Barry Feinberg (BF)

BOOKS:
African Way, The, Mike Boon, Zebra, 1996
Beyond the Barricades, Popular resistance in South Africa in the 1980's, Kliptown books, 1991 (BF)
Bram Fischer, Afrikaner Revolutionary, Stephen Clingman, David Philip, 1997
Chained Together, Mandela, De Klerk and the Struggle to Remake South Africa, David Ottaway (Random House) 1993
Habla Nelson Mandela, Pathfinder Press, NY USA, 1986 (SAL)
In the Words of Nelson Mandela, edited by Jennifer Crwys-Williams, Penguin, 1998
Legacy of Apartheid, The, edited by Joseph Harker, *Guardian* newspapers, 1994
Long Walk to Freedom (autobiography) Nelson Mandela, MacDonald Purnell, 1994
Mandela, Ronald Harwood, Channel 4, 1987 (SAL)
Mandela, Echoes of an Era, Alf Kumalo, text by Es'kia Mphahlele, Penguin, 1990, (SAL)
Mandela's Five years of Freedom: South African Politics, Economics and Social Issues, 1990–1995, compiled by Elna Schoeman, Jacqueline A Kalley and Naomi Musiker, SAIIA, Biographical series no. 29, Vol. 10, 1996 (SAL)
Nelson Mandela, Mary Benson, Penguin Books, 1986
Nelson Mandela and Apartheid, Petero Nangoli, New Horizon, 1978, (SAL)

Nelson Mandela and the rise of the ANC, Jürgen Schadeberg, Jonathan Ball and AD Donker Publishers, 1990 (SAL)
Nelson Mandela Speaks, David Philip, Mayibuye Books and Pathfinder, 1993 (BF)
Nelson Mandela Speeches 1990, Intensify the Struggle to Abolish Apartheid, edited by Greg McCartan, Pathfinder Press, 1990
Nelson Mandela, symbol of resistance and hope for a free South Africa, edited by ES Reddy, Namedia Foundation, Sterling Publishers, New Delhi, India, 1990 (SAL)
Nelson Rolihlahla Mandela, Two Historic Speeches, Learn and Teach Publications, 1990
Opposition in South Africa, the leadership of ZK Matthews, Nelson Mandela and Stephen Biko, Tim M Juckes, Praeger, 1996
Patterns of Violence, Case Studies of Conflict in Natal, edited by Anthony Minnaar, HSRC Publishers, 1992
Robben Island, Charlene Smith, Struik and Mayibuye Books, 1997 (and associated interviews and research)
Robben Island, the Reunion, Mayibuye Books, 1996
Satyagraha in South Africa, Mohandas Gandhi, Navajivan Publishing House, Ahmedabad, 1928
Struggle for Liberation in South Africa, The, Govan Mbeki, Mayibuye and David Philip, 1992
Sunset at Midday, Govan Mbeki, Nolwazi, 1996
Walden on Heroes, BBC, 1998

RESOURCE MATERIALS:
Agreements entered into between the African National Congress and the South African government at the summit meeting held on 26 September 1992 (SAL)
ANC London, Box 50 (MC)
ANC, Lusaka conference reports 1985. (MC)
ANC Lusaka Secretary-General NEC (ILC) meetings 1990 to 1991 (52.1 to 52.6) (MC)
ANC Lusaka, Secretary General NEC (NWC) Minutes, 1986 to 1990 (51.1 to 51.5) (MC)
ANC National preparatory committee documents of the National Consultative Conference, Lusaka, 1985 (MC)
ANC NEC January 8 statement, 1996, delivered by Nelson Mandela
ANC NEC statement, January 8, 1991, delivered by deputy president, Nelson Mandela (SAL)
Dawn, journal of Umkhonto we Sizwe, MK 25th anniversary (MC)
Empty Talk while the Country Burns, United democratic Front pamphlet, 1991 (SAL)
Freedom, Justice and Dignity for all in South Africa, statements and articles by Mr Nelson Mandela, president of the African National Congress of South Africa, issued by the Centre against Apartheid, Department of Political and Security Council Affairs, 1978 (SAL)
Groote Schuur Minute, The, May 1990 (SAL)
Invest in Peace, addresses by the President of the Republic of South Africa, Mr Nelson Mandela to the United Nations General Assembly and to the joint houses of the congress of the United States of America, October 1994

Is there a National Agenda – and who sets it? Thabo Mbeki, Prestige Lecture, University of Port Elizabeth, 1995 (SAL)
Land Hunger, Liberation, February, 1956 (SAL)
Letter from Nelson Mandela to Mrs Manorama Bhalla, secretary of the Indian Council for cultural relations, New Delhi, 3 August 1980 (SAL)
Letter from Dr Uwe Kaestner, the ambassador to South Africa of the Federal Republic of Germany, 27 May 1998
Message of condolence from Nelson and Winnie Mandela to the Mozambican people, the Machel family, Frelimo and the Mozambican government on the occasion of the death of Samora Machel, October 1986 (SAL)
Nelson Mandela addresses the Special Committee Against Apartheid, United Nations, 22 June 1990 (SAL)
Nelson Mandela, letter 3 August 1980, on Acceptance of the Jawaharlal Nehru Award for International Understanding for 1979, United Nations Centre Against Apartheid (SAL)
Nelson Mandela, The People's Leader, issued by UNB, MSRC, an Asoso affiliate, 1983 (SAL)
No Easy Walk to Freedom, presidential address by Nelson R Mandela, ANC (Transvaal), 21 September 1953 (SAL)
People are destroyed, Liberation, October, 1955 (SAL)
Pretoria Minute, The, 6 August 1990 (SAL)
South Africa's Freedom Struggle, Yusuf Dadoo, Kliptown books, 1990
Shifting Sands of Illusion, The, Liberation, June 1953 (SAL)
Slovo The Unfinished Autobiography, Ravan Press, 1995
Tribute to Nelson Mandela, by Mac Maharaj, 4 June 1998
University of Zimbabwe, Addresses and Orations on the occasion of the conferment of the degree of Doctor of Law on Nelson Rolihlahla Mandela, 6/7 June 1986 (SAL)

INTERVIEWS, DISCUSSIONS:
My own files, notebooks and tape recordings of interviews, discussions, meetings, conferences and the ilk over more than two decades of journalism.
- Interviews Amin Cajee, since 1986
- Interviews Helen Joseph since 1982
- Various Nelson Mandela, since 13 February 1990, and also press conferences
- Indres Naidoo, 2 , 8, 9 June 1998
- Parliament, 3 June 1998
- Alan Fine, 8 June 1998
- Su Vos, 8, 15 June 1998
- Jay Naidoo, 8 June 1998
- Zamindlela Zama, 15 June 1998
- Patrick Lekota, 9 June 1998
- Barry Streek, 10 June 1998
- Mangosuthu Buthelezi, 9 June 1998
- Truth and Reconciliation Commission hearings into chemical and biological warfare, Cape Town, 10, 11, 12 June 1998
- Govan Mbeki, 12 June 1998
- Archbishop Desmond Tutu, 18 June 1988